Praise for
REBECCA LYNN POPE AND TH

"As my dating coach, Rebecca has helped me at each phase of this process–offering feedback, helping me develop clarity on my values and preferences, and coaching me through unforeseen issues that have arisen along the way. She is more than my dating coach, she is my life coach. She speaks very openly and honestly about all aspects of my life and constantly challenges me to grow as an individual. Within a month of working with Rebecca, I am meeting and dating again after 5 years. I no longer feel like it's impossible, I am enjoying the moment, for the first time in my life." — Shanetta Brown

"I could never thank God enough for allowing me to meet Rebecca Lynn. She is the most amazing person, with the purest heart of anyone that I've ever met; her presence makes me feel like everything is OKAY even when it's falling apart right in front of me. Before meeting Rebecca I was lost and at my lowest point still suffering from past hurt, but because of her, I've been able to face, heal, and overcome some of my darkest days. She made me want to be the best version of myself and accepted me even when I didn't accept myself. I could never express how much I love, respect and genuinely thank her for being my light in such dark places." — Lacreisha Griffin

"I met Rebecca virtually through joining the online Godly Girls Club. Rebecca was such a genuine and kindhearted individual who set the tone for the group, members, and events. I became one of her coaching clients through completing the Healed to Love course which was amazing and full of revelation. Although I found love, I continue as one of her coaching clients and Divine Dreamers because I have more areas of my life to obtain abundance and manifest more greatness." — Dr. Fenisa Flowers

"I remember the day I registered for Rebecca's 7 Steps to Love course. I was excited but a little apprehensive. The weeks following I prayed, reaffirmed, cried, surrendered & let it all go. I had someone right there with me... praying for & with me, facing my fears and concerns with me. Today I'm closer to God than I've ever been. What I learned & gained was much more than I could have ever imagined. Her love, support & transparency has been a blessing. Taking the 7 Steps to Love course was a turning point in my life. I don't plan on looking back." — TiJuan Mosley

"When I joined Godly Girls, I was broken and defeated. I was in a lifeless marriage. Rebecca Pope inspires the hopeless and rejuvenates the spirit in you. She's tough, firm, yet loving at the same time. She holds you accountable for your own actions. The Godly Girls Club gave me affirmation and confirmation I was on the right track."
— LaVonda Morgan

"Last year I felt like my life was spiraling out of control. I was unsure of my purpose and felt so defeated. The moment I connected with Rebecca, I knew she was a God send. I felt like she loved me and wanted the best for me. I immediately signed up for the "7 Steps to Love" course. Rebecca coached me back to completely loving myself. I've been able to forgive myself and let go of past hurts. My whole life has shifted. I've found love and aligned myself with a group of positive, loving women in the Godly Girls Club."

— Shequoia Holloway

"Before I met Rebecca Lynn Pope, I was walking around broken, lonely, despondent and confused. On the outside, I masked the internal turmoil I was feeling: shame, guilt, and worthlessness. I was struggling to exist. I suffered a great deal with depression, anxiety, and low self-esteem. I felt daily a sense of hopelessness. Joining Godly Girls led me to a path of healing. I have gained many sisters and friendships through the Godly Girls Club that I could not dream of one year ago. I feel confident, loved and I am pursuing by purpose as designed by God." — Cheryl L. Clark

"As a client of Rebecca's, I can attest to her being a natural giver of her time and gifts. She has the strong ability to stir up God-given gifts that try to lie dormant but to no effect. The anointing on her life connects with your heart, and the healing begins. I thank God for her transparency and her life-story, which in some ways is the story of many. She labors in love so that others can receive LOVE." — Monica Walters

"Rebecca Lynn Pope is truly living on Purpose! She is a tell-it-like-it-is coach that leads with love and has an undeniable gift for helping others to find and live on purpose. Since joining the Godly Girls Club and receiving her outpouring of encouragement and guidance along with actionable goals, I have seen my hearts desires manifest like never before! She is a blessing to us all." — Vangi Caver

"The Healed to Love course has been eye-opening and life-changing for me. I don't care how well read, well versed or successful you THINK you are this course is essential and NEEDED. I came out on the other side with passion, purpose and the ability to push past obstacles!" — Dr. Keri Norris

"I often wonder if Rebecca has any idea of how she helped me. She encouraged me to stop procrastinating and move...she made an introduction that took me from being a cleaning lady to the owner of a janitorial service. When I look at the stability, love, and success, I'm currently experiencing I can't help but to think of the woman who is so pretty on the outside and downright breathtaking on the inside. And I am getting married in August!" — Jamila Hamlett

"Before beginning to work with Rebecca Lynn, I was broken, unhealthy, sad, angry, and exhausted. I was in a dark place, unable to see my own self-worth. Within only a few weeks of beginning, the Healed to Love course I saw a change. She sees in what you cannot see for yourself." — Shanika Wells

"Before I began working with Rebecca Lynn, my professional and personal lives were in conflict. There were days that I opted to travel versus spend time at home with family. Rebecca reintroduced me to myself and gave me the necessary tools to not only love my current situations but to also love myself first! I am now in love and prospering."

— Jacquelyn Thomas

"Thank you, Rebecca, for walking in your purpose. We would have never met and married if it weren't for you. Continued blessings." — David & Karren Manuel

LOVE AND DATING
IN THE 21ST CENTURY

A GODLY GIRL'S GUIDE

REBECCA LYNN POPE

POPE PUBLISHING

Love and Dating in the 21st Century

Book Design by Tamlyn Design.

ISBN (978-0-9987539-2-8)

For my mother, Linda, you were a shining example of humility, love, and grace. For my father, Charles, the first man to love me, thank you for protecting and providing for me. For my sons, I love you with all my heart and believe in you. And for my husband, Kerry A. Pope, it seems I waited forever for you to come and now that you are here, I am so grateful for all of your love and support. I love you with all of my heart and soul. And finally, for all the single women who desire to be married, I pray this book helps you on your personal journey to abundant life and love.

CONTENTS

INTRODUCTION

I haven't always been deeply in love and happily married. For the longest time, it seemed I was doomed to be forever single. For many years I was a single matchmaker, the worst possible scenario because, as a relationship expert, shouldn't I have had it all figured for myself and been happily married already? Well, just like you, I had a personal journey and some lessons God was trying to teach me along the way. This book shares my journey as well as some of the observations, wisdom, and knowledge I have gained coaching and matching people over the years. My hope is this book helps you navigate the new landscape of love and dating in the 21st Century.

> *We don't get what we want in life, we get what we are ready to receive.*

1

THE FAIRY TALE

Let me prepare you for the journey we are about to go on together. First, I am a no-nonsense coach and matchmaker. I promise to always give it to you straight. I am like that best friend who tells you what you *need* to hear and not what you *want* to hear. Like that Auntie who is real and raw yet you love her to pieces because she is fun and you can count on her to always have your back. So with everything I give you in this book please know I give it to you in the spirit of love because I truly want you to be married and have abundant life. And once upon a time, maybe it was easier, but not now. So I cannot afford to sugar-coat things for you or act like we live in a fairy tale or biblical times. We live in the 21st Century, and this book will help you learn and adapt to thrive in *these* times, without sacrificing who we are as women of faith. I am going to be real and transparent, and declare this book a judgment free zone. Remember, you get what you are prepared and ready to receive. So let's do the work together to prepare you for love and dating.

A fairy tale is defined as "a children's story about magical and imaginary beings and lands; denoting something regarded as resembling a fairy story in being magical, idealized, or extremely happy. A fairy tale is a fabricated story, especially one intended to deceive."[1] Synonyms for fairy tale are a lie, fantasy, a fable, fabrication, an untruth. Is the fairy tale love women have been raised to believe actually real? Are the expectations and ideals you have about your future partner and husband realistic? I will begin with a short story...

> *A fairy tale is a fabricated story, especially one intended to deceive.*

Once upon a time, there was a beautiful princess whose father was the most powerful and wealthy king in all of the land. The princess was loved and protected by the King and all of his men. She didn't work, ate the best food, wore the most fabulous gowns, and was admired and desired throughout the Kingdom for her beauty. The Princess dreamed of one day meeting a Prince, her very own knight-in-shining-armor, who, like her father, would protect and provide for her. Then one day, everything takes a turn for the worse, and the Princess is in serious trouble. Horrible dragons threaten the princess and the entire kingdom. Her father cannot help her. Who would rescue her? Not herself certainly, in what land do women do that? Why it's her dream Prince of course! The Prince mysteriously appears to rescue the Princess. They kiss and wed in the most fabulous ceremony and live happily ever after!

You may be laughing to yourself however we women are programmed with these types of stories from birth. These stories, in different variations and forms, repeatedly reinforce the same message: women are objects of beauty, our only purpose is to be wives and mothers; men are to protect and provide for us because we are the weaker sex, and we cannot provide for ourselves. These stories are weaved into our psyche and reinforced daily in such a way that we don't realize it is impacting our expectations of men, marriage, and dating. But when was the last time you were rescued by a man or anyone for that matter? Most women I know have to work and can't sit around eating bonbons all day choosing which dress to wear next, and that includes the wives. In fact, I don't know anyone in real life that this story fits.

It certainly doesn't describe me. The first person I met wasn't my happy ending, and since you are reading this book, my guess is yours wasn't either. I have had to slay a dragon or two in my real life, and no one was around to rescue me. And I had definitely kissed a few frogs before I met my Prince Charming but that is about as close as my life gets to resembling a fairy tale. Although fairy tales are not real, I know God desires all of us to have an abundant life. Abundant life has five elements: health, wealth, love, peace, and purpose. Love is only one element of an abundant life. However it is vital. So if you have reached a point where you feel like maybe it is just meant for you to remain single, understand that God did not create you to be alone.

If you desire in your heart to be a wife, God doesn't give a vision without giving you provision to accomplish it. However, just like health, wealth, peace, and purpose, love requires discipline and focus. To be successful in love is a process just like every other area of your life. You are going to be required to mature, change, and learn. And this is one of the biggest hurdles for women because our programming is that love is supposed to happen naturally, easily, with little to no effort on our part. This

God doesn't give a vision without giving you provision to accomplish it.

just isn't true for most of us. Approaching love and dating with fairy tale expectations will leave you very hurt and disappointed.

Like most women, my expectations and theories on love were very "fairy-tale-ish" growing up. This was reinforced through romance novels I consumed as a teenager, and some of my favorite movies such as Pretty Woman, Sixteen Candles, and Dirty Dancing. *Don't judge me, I am a hopeless romantic.* What I saw in these stories was a common denominator; all it took to be successful in a relationship was to be attracted to a man and for him to be crazy about you. So with these dreams in mind, I married very young, not once, but twice, before I was twenty-one. And when I look back, I can honestly say I was so young and dumb. I wasn't thinking about any of the crucial questions I should have asked myself before getting married. Because let's be clear, your choice in a spouse is the most important decision you will ever make in your life. It can either make or break you. You can't afford to move too fast or ignore red flags.

> *Your choice in a spouse is the most important decision you will ever make in your life.*

Now, these young men I married were good guys but by no means could they live up to the standards I had in my head. No one could live up to those standards. In my early twenties, I didn't know who I was, what I truly wanted, or where I was going, but I sure thought I had it figured out. I married with the wrong things in mind. I married based on them being cute, fun, and being crazy about me. That may work in the movies and books but, nine times out of ten, it doesn't work for most people and ends in divorce. My father was also a minister so, as a preacher's kid, I had added pressures and expectations of marriage. Dating wasn't allowed. If I am really honest, I felt pressured to get married young because "good girls" don't date or have sex outside of marriage.

Fast forward, to my early thirties, and I found myself divorced after a ten year marriage and single for the first time in my adult life. I was thrown into a world completely foreign to me. However I approached dating in much the same way I had as a teenager and in my early twenties, dating based on them being cute, fun, and how much they liked me. This was a lot of fun for a while because I learned that, when you just want fun, dating is a blast! However, when you get serious and want someone special and long-term, it suddenly becomes very difficult and complicated. *This is when I started adding more requirements and parameters around what I wanted and thought I needed.* Unfortunately, most of these requirements came from my previous experiences of what didn't work in my marriages. I used those very limited experiences upon which to base my new dating theories, something I see most people do.

One thing I was guilty of was taking what didn't work in my marriages or dating experiences and looking for the exact opposite. If I dated a man with kids and it didn't work because of the kids, I thought "I need a man that doesn't have kids." If a man were in school and didn't have a lot of time to date, I'd say "I can't date men who are in school." This goes on and on. Like me, people tend to keep building a list of restrictions and requirements during dating, thinking they are figuring it out when, in actuality, all that's happening is you're getting increasingly pickier as you become older. I often

> *For any rule you create, God has the exception.*

say that for "any rule you create, God has the exception." You can't categorize people because of one bad experience. That one experience doesn't mean all people are that way. It just means one person you met was that way.

I personally spent nine years being single off and on, putting all these theories to the test. I learned how to be a great dater but still hadn't met "The One." I refused to marry again until it was true love. I wanted my soulmate. I never wanted to get divorced again. I am grateful for my dating experiences because I learned more and more about *myself* and I met some truly incredible men. It is also how I became a relationship expert and coach and eventually a matchmaker. I found a passion for helping people heal from the wounds of love and dating and helping people learn how to date well. It led me to my purpose and passion for serving. And, when I was finally ready, it led me to the greatest love of my life, Mr. Kerry Pope (see our story in the Epilogue).

Men and women of all ages find dating difficult, but especially women. We are taught from an early age that you are not successful unless you are a wife and mother. If you examine how boys and girls are raised, however, there is a huge difference in values. Boys are not playing house or practicing to be fathers and husbands. They are raised to simply be productive. They build with blocks and play with trucks, practicing for an industrious life but nowhere is it ingrained in them that marriage is a symbol of success the way it is portrayed for young girls. So we grow up dreaming of one day being a wife and mother and comparing ourselves to this standard of success, no matter how lofty our many other accomplishments. Men do not have this double standard for success. Men see marriage as something they are expected to do when they are done playing and being boys when it is time to "settle down." In no way is marriage put on a pedestal for men and seen as the ultimate measure of success the way it is for women.

My love story is quite different from the books and movies I read as a child and teenager. In fact, it wasn't until I dropped the ideas of how it was *supposed* to be that I actually met my future husband. So let's break down for you the elements of the old fairy tale versus the modern day love story that helped give me clarity and more realistic expectations for dating in the 21st Century. Also, note how technology and contemporary gender roles have caused many of these changes.

- Fairy Tale vs. Modern -

	Fairy Tale	Modern Love Story
The Meet	A random meeting in person or personal introduction. Man initiates.	More likely to connect virtually through social media or dating site. Man initiates.
The Ask	The man asks for your phone number in person.	The man asks for your number via chat, or you offer it.
The Call and/or Text	Man calls within 24 hours.	Man texts to say "hi" before calling. Or may only text his initial communications.
Chatting	Man initiates phone calls to get to know you. And he keeps initiating.	Man makes contact a couple of times to show interest via calls and/or texts, then initiating is mutually and equally divided.
First Date	Man plans the first date to impress the woman and pays.	The date is typically a casual "meet and greet." The woman may give input.
Ongoing Dating	The man continues to do all planning and paying.	Man and woman share planning and paying for dates.
Sex	Sex is not even on the table until commitment or marriage.	People are having casual sex whenever, and with whomever.
Commitment	Man initiates the commitment conversation.	Woman or man initiates the commitment conversation.
Courting	The couple works towards preparing for marriage.	Can be ongoing without marriage as a goal.
Engagement	Man buys a beautiful ring and plans an elaborate proposal.	Man buys a ring within his budget and proposes in whatever manner suits the couple.
The Wedding	The wedding is expensive and requires a year of planning and prep.	The wedding is whatever the couple decides they mutually want.
The Marriage	The marriage has clearly defined traditional gender roles and responsibilities.	The marriage is an equal division of labor with non-traditional roles and responsibilities. A partnership.

As this comparative tables shows, connections and relations between men and women have drastically changed over time. All the traditional rules have been modified or completely dropped. So if you are playing by the old rule book or want to be "old fashioned" in your dating strategy, you will likely remain single for a very long time. Let's examine in more detail on how modern dating works.

The Meet. With everybody looking down into their phones, the old days of eyes meeting across a crowded room is highly unlikely. And do you notice that even when you are out and see a man and he sees you, he rarely will come over to introduce himself? That is a side effect of technology. And when is the last time a friend or family member personally introduced you to someone who was a viable potential partner? It is far more likely that men will see a post or picture of you on social media or on a dating site, will find you attractive, and, after checking you out (i.e., perusing all available pictures and content on your profile), will send you a virtual message. That is the modern day "Meet."

The Ask. The women I know who have as many dates as they want are positioned virtually to meet men. So if you rarely meet men while out or through friend/family introductions, then you need to be open to meeting men online. Men will initiate with you via your inbox. If you like what you see in a man's pictures and profile, you respond and exchange a few virtual messages. If there's mutual interest and he feels you are open, he will ask for your number.

The Call and Chatting. If he does not seize the opportunity to call, he is not interested or changed his mind. Which is why you should have more than one prospect. The lack of interest by one man doesn't hurt your feelings when you are actively dating and talking to several candidates. When you feel you have zero options, you tend to invest too much emotion in one man who hasn't earned it. In modern times, men often send a text first before calling. They are checking your availability to speak and making sure you gave him a real number. He may wait several days before calling you. There is no set rule for this. Men don't want to seem too eager, and they read a lot of advice that confuses them on what is best. At the end of the day, if he calls, he is interested in learning more about you. If he doesn't, he's not. Many men also send frequent texts as a form of communication. If he likes you after the initial call, he will continue to make contact a couple times, but he will expect you to initiate as well or else he will think you aren't interested.

The First Date. In the old fairy tale, a man would plan a beautiful first date consisting of a woman's favorite restaurant and/or an interest he has learned from getting to know her. This could include picking her up for the date if she is comfortable. In modern dating, however, you should never allow a stranger to pick you up from your home for a first date. You will likely be asked to "meet up" for coffee or drinks. This tends to be very casual, so you both have an opportunity to see each other and determine if there is more interest. If a man plans a more elaborate first date, it is most often something the man wants to do or try but doesn't want to do it alone. He wants a companion and/or it is part of his normal lifestyle. Or he is really attracted to you and is trying to impress you. In either scenario, the man pays for everything on a first date.

Ongoing Dating. Traditionally, if the first date goes well, more communication from the man would ensue with him planning more dates where he continues to pay for everything. In modern times, you are expected to initiate as well, help plan dates, and to offer to pay sometimes. A good rule of thumb is that you offer to pay for every third date or you plan a date and treat him. Some men will accept and some won't. A man may introduce you to his friends, family, and even children in this ongoing dating phase. Meeting his family, friends, or children does not mean he is committed to you exclusively. Things have become very casual in the 21st Century. Do not read too much into things. If the two of you have not mutually agreed to be exclusive, he is not your boyfriend.

Sex. In modern times, people are having sex whenever they want. It is a personal choice of mutual interest. There are no rules for when you first have sex. So if you want to wait, you are going to need to stick to your guns because this isn't common in contemporary dating. Men expect sex quickly because they are getting it easily. This doesn't mean you should feel pressured. Nearly everyone is doing it, even women of faith who act like they don't. So don't be surprised when he is surprised you are waiting to have sex. If you are serious about dating for the purpose of marriage, put those cookies in the cookie jar and don't take them out!

If you are serious about dating for the purpose of marriage, put those cookies in the cookie jar and don't take them out!

Commitment. In the fairy tale version, the man initiates a conversation to make things "official" and to ensure exclusivity in the relationship. In modern times, you do not have to wait around dating a man indefinitely to find out his intentions. In fact, you need to get comfortable asking questions and initiating conversations to see "where this is going." Most men are not relationship-ready or marriage-minded, so these are things you need to discover sooner rather than later so you don't waste time. Men who are just "playing" hate these types of questions which is exactly why you must ask. If you don't ask, you won't know. If both parties agree, you are now in a committed relationship.

Courting. Exclusive dating ensues. Titles such as "boyfriend," "girlfriend," "my man," and "my lady" are used. Now, this is where things can get tricky because, if you haven't done enough discovery before committing, you could be wrong in thinking this relationship is leading to marriage. In contemporary relationships, everyone doesn't want to get married. A man or woman could date someone for years and still see no need for marriage. People can be perfectly happy just being in a monogamous, committed relationship. You need to know if marriage is a goal for the man you are seeing. If marriage is a common goal, the couple continues getting to know each other and has discussions around future plans and the possibility of a combined life. At this time, you may or may not meet each other's family. This depends on the seriousness of the relationship and the closeness each individual has with family members.

Engagement. If courting has gone well in the traditional fairy tale version, the man plans for a ring and "popping the question." He plans for the special moment with a beautiful setting to surprise the woman. He may or may not include the women's family and friends. The woman loves to tell the story of how he proposed. In modern times, if courting has gone well and marriage is a common goal, the man plans for a ring. Popping the question, however, tends to be more organic without an elaborate scenario planned. This may be a simple dinner or a moment just walking in the park. It may be in the car while having a conversation. It can happen anywhere and at any time because the focus is on the love and commitment, not the "how."

The Wedding. In our dreamy story, the wedding is an extravagant affair requiring a year of planning and costs a lot. The couple may even go into debt paying for it. Today, a wedding could be extravagant, simple, and/or non-traditional. It is whatever the couple decides. They can dress however they want and play whatever music they want. They may even marry at the courthouse or elope to save money for future goals.

Together the couple figures out what works best for their "partnership."

The Marriage. Traditionally, marriage has clearly defined roles and responsibilities mostly determined by gender. Such as the woman cooks, the man takes out the trash. In modern marriages, there are defined roles and responsibilities, but the couple decides what works best for them and equally divides labor. It is a partnership. He may cook because he likes it and his schedule is more flexible. She may cut the grass and maintain the yard because she enjoys it. He may tackle bathrooms because he is a clean freak. She may make more money because women are outpacing men in education and entrepreneurship. He may handle the money and collective finances because he is better at it. Together the couple figures out what works best for their "partnership."

As we can see from this analysis, a lot has changed. We know the fairy tale has never been exactly true but why have things gotten so hard and complicated? Our parents and grandparents stayed together. Divorce used to be taboo. What happened? Why don't men approach as much? What brought about these changes? Why are traditional gender roles dying? The answer is that our options and expectations have changed.

Chapter 1 Reflections:

1. In what way have you incorporated fairy tale thinking and expectations into your love and dating life?
2. How may these false or unrealistic expectations be holding you back from being more open to the ways God may want to bless you?
3. Begin to pray and ask God to help you overcome any fears and false motivations you may have for what you expect in a man.

2

MODERN MARRIAGE

Marrying for love is a fairly modern concept. It is only within the last two hundred and fifty years that the concept of a "love match" or even marrying based on attraction has become prevalent.[2] Historically, fathers married their daughters off for the purposes of wealth, power, and alliances. Even poor people had hopes of marrying their daughters to less impoverished suitors for the good of the overall family. Girls, we were traded like property.

More recently, in the last fifty years, we are not only marrying for love and attraction, but we have also evolved to seeing marriage as a partnership with most people "now believing marriage is based on love, mutual sexual attraction, equality and a flexible division of labor."[3] The choices and freedoms in dating and marriage we now take for granted were fought hard for and have only come about in very modern times. These changes are at the core of why dating, connecting, and marriage has become so difficult. The rules and roles have changed. But why have they changed? How did marriage, and therefore dating, evolve into a spirit of love and

Marriage is based on love, mutual sexual attraction, equality and a flexible division of labor.

partnership? And how do these changes affect how we must adapt today? Let's put this in perspective by examining the history of how marriage has evolved.

Throughout history, men wrote the laws and created rules to control women and keep them in a position of submission. Marriage is an ancient institution, "It was a way of getting in-laws, of making alliances and expanding the family labor force."[4] Women were not permitted to choose their husband. A suitable husband was chosen by her family particularly by her father. Her feelings were not taken into consideration.

These alliances were about wealth, land, and family. Many cousins were married to each other to keep wealth within a family. Or daughters were forced to marry the son of a farmer with land adjacent to your family's land so water and resources could be shared. In early cultures, a man could divorce a woman if she was unable to have children and she was not permitted to remarry. However, they had no way of knowing if it was the husband or wife who had reproductive issues, in either case, it was the woman who was cast aside. Until the 19th Century, by law, men were permitted to have extramarital affairs, and women were not. A woman could not divorce her husband because he was cheating. It was simply accepted. Women during these times had no rights. Upon marriage, the husband took ownership of all land, property, and money a woman would inherit through her family. Women were seen as intellectually inferior, weaker, and often times as evil or a source of weakness for men (i.e. Adam and Eve). We were second class citizens who were only necessary for child production, so if a woman was unable to have children, she held no value. Women had to be obedient to men at all times and to not question them. The Bible and religion were used to reinforce these beliefs. Abuse was widespread but, without money, how could a woman leave an abusive husband? She would be an outcast and have no way to provide for herself or her children. Up until the 1970's, marital rape was still legal in many states.

In essence, many women were domestic slaves. Women and children were considered "virtually property by the man just like material possessions."[5] And it was only after actual slavery was abolished in the United States in 1865 that women began to receive more rights as well. Women across all races, cultures, and faith have this history in common. Sexism and racism go hand in hand. It wasn't until the end of the 19th Century that women were permitted to attend colleges and receive broad formal education, less than one hundred and fifty years ago. We didn't receive the right to vote until 1920. When the United States was formed, just like slaves, women did not receive the same rights as white men. Things began to change when women started working in larger numbers and making their own money. "From 1960 to the early 1970s the influx of married women workers accounted for almost half of the increase in the total labor force, and working wives were staying in their jobs longer before starting families."[6]

In essence, many women were domestic slaves. Women and children were considered "virtually property by the man just like material possessions".

Up until the 1970's, if you did divorce, the husband retained all rights to the property and children. It was only as women began making their own money that they were able to get out of unhappy and abusive marriages. We've still got a long way to go, however. Legislation such as the Equal Pay Act of 1963 requires equal wages for equal work for men and women, yet women still do not receive equal pay. We are discriminated against by a male dominated society that still retains many of the sexist viewpoints and practices they've had for thousands of years. Mention the word Feminism to a man, and you will get a wide range of reactions, opinions, and emotions, not all positive. Many men resent women having equal rights. In many cases, sexism is just as evil as racism.

"Feminism…the definition, as I have spent my life believing it to be, is the belief that men and women should have equal social, political, and economic rights and opportunities." ~ Theresa Younger[7]

So were there happy marriages prior to feminism and equal rights for women? Yes, of course. However, there were just as many marriages where the women felt stuck and would have left if they could. They stayed through extramarital affairs, illegitimate children, and different types of emotional, verbal, and physical abuse. Our parents, grandparents, and great-grandparents didn't all live in marital bliss. They didn't divorce because they couldn't. And it's important we think about this because we tend to look at our parents and grandparents generation as the examples for marriage. We compare the longevity of their marriages to current times and feel like things are so bad now. It is not that things are so bad. It is that we now have choices. Choices of who to love, who to marry, and the choice to divorce if we aren't happy. These are choices we never had before, and it is these options that make dating and relationships so complicated in modern times.

> *Our parents, grandparents, and great-grandparents didn't all live in marital bliss.*

One dramatic result of the choices we now have is that people are getting married less and less because we no longer have the financial and physical pressures to do so. We don't need men to hunt and gather and fight for us. If a burglar breaks into your house with a gun right now, is a man any better equipped to protect you physically than you could protect yourself? Men and women are becoming more and more equal. With all of these changes, marriage is not even a goal for many. So if you desire marriage, you have to adopt a new mindset and position which is centered in partnership.

> *So if you desire marriage, you have to adopt a new mindset and position which is centered in partnership.*

First, not all men are ready for marriage or even want marriage, and there is absolutely nothing you can do to make a man ready. Men now get all the benefits of marriage without any of the responsibilities. It isn't even about meeting the right woman because he can know you are phenomenal yet still not be ready to be married. Once they are ready, however, it is like a light switch goes from off to on and they start dating with the purpose of finding a wife. So love and marriage have more to do with timing and values than anything else because a man can love you and still not be ready for marriage. Women tend to think they are ready because of our conditioning for love and marriage. However, not all women are innately ready for a healthy relationship either.

It has only been in the last fifty years that women have shifted from being housewives and mothers to being financially independent of men. And this affects the very foundation of our traditional beliefs about marriage. As women living in the 21st Century, we still want men to be the providers and protectors because it is what we have been raised to believe we should look for in a husband by our mothers and grandmothers. However, if we are honest, our mothers, grandmothers, and great-grandmothers were not all happy women. Many suffered and struggled and sacrificed their lives, purpose, desires, and dreams for us. They did it for us!

They did not have the freedoms we have to marry for love and partnership. They were not able to get degrees, start companies, write books, or travel the world. Their passions, intelligence, and drive were not allowed to flourish. Many stayed in unhappy marriages even after they could have left to hold their families together. Many women became institutionalized in their thinking. Although freedom came, they still didn't feel free to leave. They were still imprisoned by low self-esteem, fear, and doubt that they could survive and thrive on their own. I know this resonates with many of you just like it does with me.

We all have sisters, friends, aunts, mothers, and grandmothers who are still in these situations. They are unhappy and often abused mentally, verbally, or physically. They should have left years ago yet stay because it is all that they know. Many have a mindset centered on receiving their blessings in heaven while living in hell on earth. Men have manipulated and torn down these women. As women, we have to understand that we have inherited a lot of this antiquated thinking. We have put limits and expectations on ourselves that no longer fit who we are now nor God's best for our lives. Our

> *Our foremothers did not have the jobs, finances, power, and opportunities we have. We cannot continue to choose men based on their old mindset and limited choices.*

foremothers did not have the jobs, finances, power, and opportunities we have. We cannot continue to choose men based on their old mindset and limited choices.

We don't turn around thousands of years of abuse and control within fifty years. We women cannot take our new liberty for granted. We have to exercise our right to choose a man for love and true compatibility. We have to be bold and embrace our power, abilities, and strengths to strike out on our own and only love and marry a man who is a true purpose partner and soulmate. A man who contributes to your happiness and enhances your life. Our mothers and grandmothers fought to give us this right. They didn't just fight for equal rights in employment, politics, and social justice. They fought for our right to choose love.

One observation of the hundreds of clients who have come to me, is men and women are both trying to figure out the balance between desiring love in a relationship yet still fulfill the traditional values we have inherited from our families, religion, and society. As a matchmaker, I come face-to-face with the effects of the traditional mindset clashing with our modern roles as successful and independent women. When I started the agency, I accepted male and female clients. However, ninety-nine percent of my clients were women. These women were predominantly lawyers, doctors, or upper-level executives with low six-figure incomes. One hundred years ago women wouldn't have these types of positions and careers, and that puts them in a very unique position of trying to balance professional and financial success with the social pressures they feel to be wives and mothers.

Over the years, I began seeing a trend. The majority of these women had created an "ideal mate" in their head who was a combination of the old traditional requirements based on when we needed men to be providers and protectors with new additional preferences that fit modern times. When a woman of this caliber requires a man to be a "good provider," it often equates to a man meeting or exceeding her income. Also, they want a man who is their equal socially, economically, physically, and so on. Every potential match was weighed and measured against this ideal. What I found is there are not enough men who match these women dollar-for-dollar who also match all their other preferences.

The 21st Century fairy tale man – this idyllic mate – is making six to seven figures and significantly upgrades the woman's current life financially. He is six foot or taller and very good looking (think Idris Elba or Matthew McConaughey). He is spiritually mature and prepared to lead a woman. He values family and is a complete gentleman. He never loses his temper and is sensitive to a woman's needs and feelings. He is attentive, and you can talk to him about anything just like your girlfriends. He is someone who makes you the envy of all your friends, and you love showing him off. He is kind, smart, and hardworking. If you decide to have kids, working will become an option, not a requirement, because he's got you covered financially. He is faithful and loyal. He loves his mother but isn't a momma's boy, and he knows how to put her in her place to protect his woman. He doesn't have a criminal record, has never been to jail, and has great credit. I could go on ad nauseam with this description.

There is a huge problem with this fairy tale man, though, they don't exist. And if he did, it is unlikely he would want you because he can have whoever he wants. On a scale of one to ten, this man is a twenty. And these men don't tend to want the super driven, workaholic, independent woman, they want the super gorgeous and catering woman. Just like women have been brainwashed to want the "Alpha Male Provider-type," men have been indoctrinated for thousands of years to want a woman who is flexible to his schedule, catering to his needs, more submissive in nature, and strokes his ego.

These men who seemingly are the entire package can have whoever they want because there are so few of them yet there is an endless supply of pretty women who would cater to him. And as we age, there are fewer and fewer men available who meet even half of these criteria. Let's be honest, *you* don't meet half these criteria. Many of my clients have been holding out for Mr. Perfect and remain perpetually single. A thirty-five-year-old woman who is holding out for this perfect guy could be waiting a very long time.

One of the number one complaints I hear from women is men are not the hunters anymore. They don't pursue or initiate. My answer is because they don't have to be. The rules of engagement have completely changed. This is a side effect of feminism and technology. We wanted to be treated as equals, so we've got it. Men now think, why should I have to approach a woman? Why can't she approach me? Why do I have to pay for everything, she makes just as much money or more money than me? We can't rewind the clock. What's done is done. We can no longer expect things to work the way they used to when everything else has changed. We don't get to pick and choose what aspects of the old world we want to hang on to while operating in the new world. We can, however, find a balance between the old and new. And I'll tell you how in this book.

Chapter 2 Reflections:

1. How does understanding the history of marriage help you adjust your thinking about gender roles today?
2. Do you agree that modern marriage works best as a partnership?
3. Is this how you want your marriage to operate?

3

TECH NOLOGY AND SOCIAL MEDIA

I met my husband via Facebook. Ten years ago I wouldn't have had the opportunity to tell my personal love story because Facebook wasn't mainstream and I likely wouldn't have met my husband through traditional means. It wasn't until 2009 that I began using Facebook daily. Fast forward to 2016, and it has a billion users and growing. Ten years ago we also didn't have online social groups like Meetup.com and Facebook groups, dating apps, chat messenger, video calling, or smart phones, all combining to create an almost unlimited ability to connect with people worldwide. Technology has changed the entire landscape of dating. People are still connecting, but those connections are happening in new ways.

> *Technology has changed the entire landscape of dating.*

> *Seven out of ten long-term relationships, or relationships that lead to marriage, are initiated through an online platform.*

There is no going back from this monumental transition. Through my own research, I estimate that seven out of ten long-term relationships, or relationships that lead to marriage, are initiated through an online platform. This includes social media such as Facebook, Instagram, and Twitter as well as the thousands of dating sites and apps. I even hear love stories from people connecting on LinkedIn which historically has only been for professional business networking. High school and college friends are reconnecting on Facebook. People are direct messaging for love on Instagram. Wherever people are in large numbers, they will find a way to connect. Love is a powerful and motivating force. It is a basic human need.

Social media, in particular, has drastic effects on the psychology of people. "According to this latest research, people in the U.S. check their Facebook, Twitter, and other social media accounts a staggering 17 times a day and spend an average of 4.5 hours a day on their phones"[8]. The effect of this much time on social media is that it has shrunk the world. We now can go online at any time and see thousands of people's pictures, details of their personal lives, and peek into their thoughts. This makes us feel like we know these people when, in fact, we don't really know these people at all. We never meet them in real life and only see what they choose to share. We are in essence seeing highlight reels of people's lives and given access on a level that we only used to see with celebrities.

Everyone now has a "personal platform" to be perceived however they want. This further reinforces our fairy tale mindset and has us comparing ourselves to "fake" virtual lives. This psychology has us trying so hard to mimic in real life these Photoshopped moments of perfection. We are all trying to be thinner, richer, happier, and successful. This includes our love lives. Your ideal dating scenario and wedding is probably greatly influenced by these images without you even realizing it. And the problem is these images only tell one side of the story. You don't know who these people really are. Or what they have had to sacrifice to get there. Often if you hear their personal stories, you would be very unwilling to suffer through it to have what they have.

As we spend increasingly more time on social media, we are becoming more detached from reality and less truly connected. People are doing all types of crazy things for "likes" in order to connect because they are sharing the most intimate details of their life. When it comes to dating, that sense of intimacy also causes people to feel like have more options. Men are very visual creatures, and social media provides an endless supply of eye-candy. As men follow women's online "oversharing," they begin to feel as if they are really getting to know these women. And, unlike celebrities, they believe these gorgeous women are just "everyday gals" who are accessible and dateable. They don't realize many of these women (i.e., model/vixen/actress type) wouldn't give the average man the time of day. These women are dating and/or sleeping with very wealthy men, handsome men, pro-athletes, and rappers. Nonetheless, the lines become very blurred between what these men think they deserve or can have when it comes to beautiful women.

These men then pursue women who are out of their league and experience rejection or get used for their money. After a couple cycles, these men begin calling women "gold-diggers," however it is not all women who are gold-diggers, it is just the women they are choosing. They overlook all of the smart, hardworking, faithful women chasing these "gorgeous" women who have zero interest in them, and steadily complain about the lack of good women. This is just one of social media's effects on dating, false expectations. So many men you will meet are hurt and damaged. They have given opportunities and offered their hearts to the wrong women just like you have done with men.

Social media is just as bad for women but in a different way. We are constantly bombarded with images of picture perfect relationships, proposals, and weddings. We now have male relationship experts that are super fine and feed us messages all day of what men should and shouldn't be doing for you, how "real men" need to treat you, and in the meantime, you don't realize you are being played. These gorgeous buff men are often just telling you what you want to hear to help you feel better about being single while they sell you another book or workshop. And mind you, they aren't married, committed, or doing all the things they preach. But you fall for it, hook-line-and-sinker, and just keep adding all these requirements to your long list of "needs" and "non-negotiables," while fantasizing this dream guy looks just like your favorite male relationship expert. It is smoke and mirrors gals. If you want to be married, take advice from a married man or woman, or least someone who is very happy in a relationship and lets it be known.

We rub virtual elbows with hunky men all over social media and in affinity groups too. And by doing so, we begin to believe that our future man can look like Mr. 6'4" Sexual Chocolate that's in your favorite group. Or shoot, he could even be The One. You feel all that virtual flirting is really going somewhere until you learn he has slept will half the women in your city and has zero interest in settling down.

Often we learn this way too late after you have fallen for the beautiful smile with very little substance to support it. You went out to eat a few times, and in your mind, this is really going somewhere. These men know exactly what to say to make you drop your guard. I listen to women describe these men as "courting" them. He is not courting you love, he is seducing you. If you knew how many women he is giving the same treatment, you would not feel so special. And God forbid you make the mistake of sleeping with him and then start asking questions about commitment or "where this is going." Be prepared for the perfectly crafted escape plan he has waiting for you. The conversation will go like this, "I am just not at a good place right now, and I have a lot on my plate." "You deserve so much more than what I can offer you." As he exits stage left. And many of you still think these men are good guys until you find out who else they have slept with in your circle of friends. You don't realize that, once again, you have been played.

One of the biggest causes for women being so gullible is their lack of dating options and inexperience. Many men have been juggling women for years. They become pros at avoiding questions and misdirection. When it comes to dating, most women are amateurs. Many of you rarely meet men you are interested in so when the seemingly perfect handsome guy comes along and shows you interest, you jump too fast and fall for the game. You don't take the time to get to know him because you have minimal dating experience and are not wise when it comes to men. You give too much, ignore red flags, and create this ideal scenario of the guy in your head – ideals not based in reality because you don't even know these dudes or collect enough information upon which to base accurate opinions. The reality is, you are more in love with the fantasy in your head, the love story you want than you are with the actual man. We try to make men fit our perfect storylines.

You are more in love with the fantasy in your head, the love story you want than you are with the actual man.

We are only deceiving ourselves. Yet, when they don't measure up, and you start seeing the truth, these men become liars, cheaters, and dogs. Are they really though? Or did you just dumb yourself down and ignore the signs? Or did you ignore everything he was trying to tell you and show you along the way? Why didn't you take the hint when he would disappear for long periods of time? The answer is because you didn't want to see it. He is not your man or boyfriend just because you went on a few dates or slept with him. And if he tells you he isn't ready for a relationship, believe him. The reasons don't matter. You can't change him, heal him, or fix him if he doesn't want to commit.

In short, ladies, be careful of these popular, gorgeous guys on social media. If he has that much time to be on social media, he's likely not focusing enough on things that really matter, and he isn't the type of man you want anyway. Tons of women are trying to get with him, and he is not ready to settle down.

Which brings me to dating. You have to date! You need options. When you have options, you won't entertain clowns, and you will see things more clearly. You know how you are supposed to be treated and you know what it looks and feels like when a man is truly into you. The only way I know for you to access options and begin dating more is online dating. There are literally millions of men online. I know many of you have tried and literally hate online dating. And if that is you, I will simply tell you…you weren't doing it right. There are great men online. You just need to know how to position yourself to meet them and to be attractive to them. I tell clients constantly, you have to fish with the right bait!

If you wonder why men don't approach women anymore, it is largely because of online dating and social media. Men never liked approaching women. It sucks. Think about it girls, a man has to walk up to you not knowing if you are married, taken, nice, mean, or anything. It takes a lot of nerve. And most of the time they get rejected. If you are honest, you have seen how your friends act when they are approached by someone they don't like. Some women are outright vicious. This might even be you. If you were a man, would you want to approach random strangers with the great possibility of humiliation? I wouldn't. So technology has made this an even playing field. It is so much easier for a gent to send you a virtual message than to approach you in person. Maybe you respond, maybe you don't, but at least he tried without the risk of you destroying his ego. So part of you getting positioned to date in the 21st Century is being open to all the different ways you could meet someone.

This also includes being open to the many ways people now communicate. Texting, instant messaging, direct messaging, Skype, Facetime, Whatsapp, email, I could go on and on. People are busy. Talking on the phone is not always feasible. My advice is to view texting just like someone passing you a note in class. It simply means they are thinking of you. My rule of thumb for communication is that if I begin to type more than three sentences as a response or initial message, then it needs to be a phone call. I refuse to hold entire conversations via text. However, short little notes are awesome! They don't replace talking but is a great addition to make dating more fun, flirty, and interactive. Who doesn't love a good morning text? That is the best. So be open to these different ways of communicating. And even send your own good morning text messages. Don't be afraid to initiate sometimes once a rhythm of communication has been established. He has made clear his interest in words and actions. Now the ball is in your court, your husband is looking for you and waiting for you.

- Online Dating -

There are approximately 54,250,000 single people in the United States. Of these, 49,250,000 have reported trying online dating.[9] That is approximately ninety-one percent of singles, and those are only the singles who reported it. Technology has completely changed how people are connecting. Match.com alone has over twenty-five million members, and fifty-two percent of them are men![10] That's right, MEN! So, at any given time, there are literally millions of single men – and opportunities – on any given dating site, who you would normally never meet and cross paths with in real life.

These statistics help explain and reinforce my logic for why men no longer feel pressured to approach women in public. It is much easier for them to simply message one of the millions of women on a dating site. Also, the site gives him pictures of you with pertinent information such as your religion, age, and interests. The complaint I often hear from men and women about dating sites is that people lie. Well, yes, sometimes they do. However, people lie in person too. There is nothing happening on a dating site that isn't happening in real life. It is just people. There are good people with good intentions, and there are not such good people with less than great intentions. That's life.

You need to be open to all possibilities. Your husband is looking for you and waiting for you. So check your ego and get with the times. Ladies, there could be a man who is only one or two degrees of separation from you right now. He is a friend of a friend

Your husband is looking for you and waiting for you.

or coworker. He is on a dating site right now wondering if you truly exist, hoping he meets you soon. Your future husband who is perfect for you is literally that close. If you aren't doing online dating, it is time to start. Get a dating coach like myself to learn what to do and what not to do. It is an art that comes naturally to some and not others, like flirting. Open your eyes and your heart because you just don't know how God is going to bless you. That day I met my husband through Facebook I had no idea he would be my forever, but I was open to an adventure, are you?

Chapter 3 Reflections:

1. In what ways is social media affecting your perceptions of love and relationships?
2. Is it contributing to unrealistic standards for men and love?
3. Are you giving yourself enough options in dating?
4. How does your perspective need to change to be open to love?

4

THE INDEPEN DENT WOMAN

What is an independent woman in modern times? As I have mentioned, one of the biggest factors affecting modern dating and marriage is the shift of women's roles in society. In the 21st Century, women don't need a whole lot of saving and rescuing. Women are outdistancing men in education. We are starting businesses at rates that run circles around men. We graduate in higher numbers and are competing for the best jobs. All of this gender equality throws gender roles out the window because women haven't historically competed with men professionally or financially.

Finances are at the heart of the gender roles shift. Historically women have depended on their fathers and husbands for financial provision. When women began working and wages began increasing is when things really started to change. Because if women are no longer dependent on their fathers and men for survival and we work just as hard, if not harder than men, then innately we want fair and equal treatment in relationships as well. So if you are working, providing and/or contributing to your family, by definition, you are an independent woman whether you want to be or not. You may still want to be a wife and mother however very few women have the option or desire to be full-time, stay-at-home mothers in their marriages. Even if you want to, the economic pressures it puts on a family are astronomical. We now live in a society that is dependent on both men and women in the workplace because it has become increasingly difficult to have a fulfilling lifestyle on one income. Roles have changed out of necessity. Women can't do it all anymore and neither can men. We both need each other. It is very challenging for a woman to work a career and maintain the household and children by herself. The average man can't be the sole breadwinner and make all the leadership decisions in a household without his wife's help.

So both women and men are left to try and figure out what's appropriate, what works and doesn't work, and what the opposite sex truly wants. I find most people, men, and women, want to pick and choose what aspects of historically traditional roles they want from the opposite sex while ditching the reverse expectations that those same rules would put on themselves. For instance, if a man wants his wife to take care of all childcare and household duties, his traditional reciprocal role is to be the sole provider; however, many men do not want or cannot support this lifestyle. This example illustrates why dating and relationships have become so difficult. People are trying to keep the old rules that benefit them while incorporating new rules that also benefit them. It is a win-win for the individual but useless because no one is going to sign up for such a lose-lose scenario and your ridiculous expectations.

Women want men to still take on the primary traditional gender roles such as provider, protector, and leadership; however, they don't want the primary responsibility of cooking and cleaning which accompanies the reverse of that ideology. Men, on the other hand, do the same thing. They want women to still cook, and take care of the children; however, they prefer more of a partnership when it comes to finances. In fact, in all of the modern marital responsibilities, people tend to want partnership instead of primary accountability for what would traditionally be required of them. This has created even greater expectations of the opposite sex because we not only want them to meet our conventional expectations, we now also want them to be a flexible partner in the roles we prefer not to do. It is time, therefore, that we adjust our thinking to more realistic expectations of the roles we play and expect in relationships...much of which hinges on finances.

Seventy-four percent of American women are working or employed outside the home just like men.11 In removing finances as the foundational building block of most relationships, seventy-five percent of women are, by definition, "independent" – whether they desire it or not. Some single women I coach relish in their financial freedom, impressive resumes, and achievements. Other singles have jobs because they must take care of themselves but truly desire to be a traditional stay-at-home mother. And then there are single women who are struggling to live paycheck to paycheck, yet are still considered independent by conventional standards.

Dating and connecting in the 21st Century is not easy. Even women who are actively meeting and dating men are frustrated because they still aren't meeting "The One." It requires a lot of patience because, unlike previous generations, you are now qualifying men – not on money, family, and reputation – but on love and true compatibility. So, it is not that things have become harder; it is that our expectations of relationships are *higher* because we now want love as well.

For all the Independent Women – which is most of us – I dedicate this chapter to you. We are choosing our own path in life, making our own money, and desire true love. We are not women who are looking to be rescued or saved by a man. We don't look at men as a solution to our problems. What we desire is unconditional love, acceptance, companionship, and partnership. We don't "need a man" just for financial reasons, we need him for love and companionship, which is a basic human need and part of abundant life.

As I have met, interviewed, coached, and matched thousands of women, I have begun to put them into categories based on why they remain single. The first category is "Alpha Females." These women use the "wish list" dating technique where they shop for the "perfect" candidate who meets a long list of requirements they have created for an ideal mate. Their married friends or friends in relationships tell them they're too picky. However, to the alpha female, being with anyone less than the ideal man in her head is "settling," and she is not a settler.

The second category of women is the "Good Girls." They are women who don't date at all or try it and then stop. They don't want to have to date. They put love on the shelf and often attribute it to "waiting on God." They focus completely on family, friends, achievements, and goals while ignoring their needs for love and companionship. Good girls struggle to adapt to dating because of their strong moral and religious beliefs as well as their "fairy tale" approach.

My final category is the "Wounded Women." These are women who have deep pain and have been damaged by life. Often alpha females and good girls are also wounded, so become a combination of two types of women. As you read about each category, think about where you fit and why you may be single.

- Alpha Females -

Alpha females are the go-getters. They are CEOs, lawyers, doctors, executives, and overall high achievers. They are smart and self-driven. They dream big and work hard. The alpha female, wants a man to match her drive and success, or if she hasn't quite achieved it yet, she wants a man who represents where she wants to go and who she wants to be. Let's use, for example, a woman who makes $150,000 a year as a small business owner and works sixty hours a week. Her position requires her to be a leader, super confident, decisive, and powerful. She will tend to want an "Alpha Male" who she feels matches these characteristics. He should be making as much money or even more than her, which means he is probably working as much if not harder than her. She tends to be very competitive because this innate trait is what has propelled her to succeed in business, get her education, and achieve her goals. This competitiveness also contributes to caring about what others think of her. She wants her spouse to increase or at least match her social equity and image, and represent her well to friends, family, and colleagues. Together, she wants to be a power couple and, subconsciously, be the envy of those around her.

All of this and we haven't even touched on her wish list of physical traits, such as over six foot, handsome, nice smile, not too fat, not too thin, and on and on. Then add in specific "needs" for education, faith, family history, hobbies, and interests. Can you begin to see how this thinking and exhaustive list of requirements is backing the alpha female into a permanently single corner? It is easy to see why so many super successful women remain single year after year because, to be honest, there just aren't enough single men who meet all these requirements. Most men who meet even half are either already married or are serial bachelors because they are so desirable to women that they are having too much fun to settle down. The number one mistake alpha females make is ignoring love in their twenties or marrying for the wrong reasons earlier in life. They put love on the back-burner or didn't cultivate love in their younger years by building success with someone. This puts them in the precarious situation of trying to meet someone who is already successful.

Add to this fact that most men do not reach the equivalent level of success without the help of a woman. So alpha males don't tend to stay single for long or, if they do, it is because they have other issues that are interfering with commitment. Hence, they still aren't fit for what alpha females want because they aren't relationship-minded. So most alpha females find themselves dating and looking for the proverbial unicorn or needle in a haystack because their ego will not allow them to just be with a man who makes them happy.

Alpha males and alpha females aren't even compatible. They are both too busy, self-involved, and consumed by work and ambition. Instead of an alpha male prototype, these women need a man who is more domesticated and laid back to help balance out her life. Alpha females are being influenced by antiquated, traditional thinking and now have added pressures of comparing men to their own personal success and achievements. It is only in modern times that women have had to balance all this because it is only in the last fifty to one hundred years that large numbers of women are making this kind of income and reaching these levels professionally. This lack of dependence on men is shifting the entire landscape of love and relationships.

It is time, therefore, that our thinking around dating and

marriage evolve as well. Women tend to want men to be the strong leader, provider, and protector and there is nothing wrong with that. However, if it also means he must match you dollar-for-dollar when it comes to income, you are going to have some problems. Most men are not making $150,000 plus a year. In fact, the average income for men over twenty-five with a bachelor's degree is $62,000. And this is just income, what about all the other requirements she has such as race, height, religion, interests, and values. She is backing herself into a corner where no one is going to meet these standards. As I have interacted with more and more alpha females, what I see is that they don't realize what they truly need. What they need is a partner. Not a fairy tale rescuer or knight in shining armor. They need a man who helps them balance their life with fun and family, which doesn't necessarily include income or professional equality.

Now before you get all worked up, I am not saying you need to settle for some low-life loser. What I am saying is holding the bar so high does not equate to love and true compatibility. You can meet the most perfect man on paper with an incredible resume and still not have any chemistry. So you have wasted your time vetting for the perfect candidate to only realize you aren't even attracted to him. If this is you, I encourage you to adapt. It is time to get realistic. The perfect man may be a different race, height, or body type than what you imagined.

I've also seen a lot of women in this category reaching for more than they bring to the table. Yes, you may make six or seven figures, have great credit, own your home, drive a luxury car, and have multiple degrees but are you in shape physically? Are you pleasant to be around? Physical attraction is the first priority for men. Many alpha females have inflated egos. They believe they deserve the very best of the best when it comes to a man and that belief is rooted in their financial and professional accomplishments, which is a very masculine way of thinking. And it doesn't work in dating because men could care less how much money you make or how many degrees you have. If they aren't attracted to you and enjoy your personality, they are not interested. Period.

Alpha women tend to want alpha men; however, the sentiment is not often reciprocated. Alpha men are not built that way. They don't want to compete with you professionally and financially. They want a relationship to be simple, fun, and enjoyable. They just want to be happy. This is why you see so many super successful men dating women who have simple jobs and don't make anywhere near what he is making. Simply put, he is more concerned with how you make him feel than your income. The average millionaire or six-figure man who comes to me for matching has no financial requirement for his matches. Their only financial requirement is the women are financially responsible. They don't want a woman who just wants to spend all their money. These men are more concerned with their matches' look and personalities. So, as much as we as women have changed, the basics of men's desires have not changed at all. They are simple. They want the sexiest woman they can get and want to live a peaceful and happy life with great sex and food. You may be laughing, but it is true.

Alpha men are setting the bar higher and higher as well, specifically when it comes to sex appeal. In a world that has become increasingly visual and image-conscious, men want a gorgeous woman who is still down-to-earth, nurturing, catering, kind, and who is not a gold-digger. In other words, they want Susie Homemaker with the body of Beyoncé. They want this even if they are overweight or older, especially men who make more money than the average man. Men with money feel very entitled to get the women they want but become very bitter when these women only find them desirable because of their money. They then categorize all women as gold-diggers when that is the position they put themselves in by not having realistic expectations. What kind of women would these men attract without money? Based on their looks, charm, wit, intellect, sense of humor, and values, what kind of woman would they be able to attract and keep? The answer is it would be a woman who was more their equal physically. She would love him for who he was, not for his money. That is a true match.

So alpha females want to marry a handsome alpha male with all their wish list qualities, while alpha males are just as satisfied with a gorgeous woman who he enjoys spending time with. We all see this when we're out – the younger gorgeous model-looking woman with the older rich-looking man. I have male matchmaking clients who are in their fifties, making six to seven figures, and, it never fails, they want to date women in their twenties and thirties. And, they will find it because there are young women who are willing to trade physical attraction for financial security. It is a double standard in our society. The game is rigged girls. The man you are holding out for doesn't even want you. They are self-centered and egotistical, and you aren't going to make him the center of your universe because you have your own endeavors. You aren't going to stroke his ego efficiently because the two of you are too much alike. This isn't going to work. You are going to have to realize all these things on your wish list are not going to make you truly happy.

The game is rigged girls.

If it sounds like I know what I am talking about, it is because I do. I am an alpha female. I am a go-getter, and I used to have a wish list a mile long. However, while dating a ton of perfect candidates, I still never found love. Many of my female clients are alpha females as well. They are my most difficult clients. We are headstrong, stubborn, and opinionated. We think we have it all figured out which makes it very difficult to change. And the predominant thinking my alpha female clients have is that they just haven't met the right alpha man yet. I can relate.

These "perfect" alpha men are never attentive enough to our needs, and often come off as controlling and needy. They always want you to drop everything for them at a moment's notice. The truth is, the workaholic, ego-driven, boss-type man is not a fit for my alpha female clients. They aren't compatible. They are too much alike. They don't make enough time for each other because they are both pursuing their dreams and endeavors. So on paper, they are a perfectly matched "power couple" but, in real life, there is no chemistry and connections. When I put these people on dates with each other, all they end up talking about is business or work. There is no deeper or spiritual connection.

Just like my clients, for me personally, it wasn't until I dropped my wish list that I met the most amazing, humble, dependable, consistent, and handsome pastor. He balances me out. He makes me stop working and focus on other things in life that matter. He is catering, loving, kind, and patient. He anchors me. He is sensitive to what I need and pays attention to all the little details. In many ways, he is so different than me, yet our hearts, goals, and visions are perfectly aligned and in one accord. He is the first man who truly has the spiritual depth my soul desires. And our sex is amazing. I wake up every day happy with my choice.

As I reflect back on my dating experiences, I remember dating an egotistical alpha male and even trying to be more domesticated and less driven. I really did try girls but, over time, I became bored out of my mind. I felt like I was dumbing myself down to be with him. I couldn't do it. He wanted me to be a full-time wife and mother and cater to his every need. I am not built that way. I broke up with him very abruptly and went right back to pursuing my dreams. I didn't care about his money, houses, or cars. His lifestyle was not enough. I couldn't change who I am to be with him. And I am so glad I didn't because I would have never met Mr. Kerry Pope. He loves and accepts me for exactly who I am.

So if you are a go-getter chick like me, it is time to drop all those ridiculous requirements and be with someone who makes you happy. You don't need his money so why not date like alpha men do? Date according to what pleases you and how he makes you feel. My clients and friends who have done this are also experiencing deep love and fulfillment in their relationships. They are crazy in love with men who are so different than what they thought they had to have in a partner.

Date according to what pleases you and how he makes you feel.

Give it a try. Begin dating men you find attractive and fun. Someone who makes you feel alive! You work really hard. You need a man who helps you to enjoy the other side of life. Someone who increases your joy and peace of mind. It is worth risking something different. I did and married someone I love waking up to every morning. He is perfect for me and fulfills needs I didn't even know I had. God knows us better than we know ourselves so, if you surrender your life to God, He will bless you in ways that you can't even imagine. I know giving up control does not come easily but, in the love department, it is the only way I know to become truly fulfilled and happy.

- Good Girls -

Another category of women are the "Good Girls." You may be a good girl if you run around saving everyone but yourself. You don't want to actively date or pursue a relationship. Good girls practically ignore their needs, including their sexuality and love life. I find this is very common with women of faith because it is very easy to tell yourself and others you are celibate because of your beliefs and that you are "waiting on your Boaz" like Ruth in the Bible because the man is supposed to "find you," not the other way around. You are not Ruth, and we don't live in the times of Proverbs 31. Unfortunately, however, it is very easy to justify and even be admired for behavior that is actually rooted in fear or the inability to adapt to modern times.

Most good girls have past hurts from men, possibly an ex-boyfriend or husband, or even a father. Many also have low self-esteem, but it is masked behind professional achievements, endeavors, and a beautiful smile. For good girls, dating multiple men feels promiscuous even if you aren't having sex. Talking on the phone with more than one man feels like cheating. They want to meet someone like our mothers and grandmothers did, through a friend or family member. They often meet one man and put all their focus, attention, and effort into him without vetting him. Often times, this leads to a string of bad relationships leaving good girls broken-hearted and hopeless about love.

Many I encounter, or who come to me for dating help, are single mothers. They literally dedicate their entire life to their professional pursuits and raising their child. And when the child is grown and ready to go to college, these women call me because they realize they need to learn how to date and can no longer ignore their love life. The ones who don't have children tend to have other causes and interests they are very dedicated to that take the place of a man in their life (i.e., sororities, church, or hobbies they love). Many have traveled extensively or are involved in volunteering or starting an organization centered on their passions. These women are all purpose-driven, but it is not balanced. They consume themselves with work, friends, and causes to not feel the absence of love from a man. If this is you, you may even try to convince yourself that you are perfectly satisfied remaining single. However, God has a way of bringing us to our truth.

We cannot forget that love is a need. And it is only one of five basic elements of having an abundant life. It doesn't matter what you accomplish, how much money you make, or how great you are as a mother, you still need and desire love. Work cannot replace affection and companionship. Your child can't replace your need for love either. Kids grow up and leave us, and we still have to deal with ourselves and our issues. If you are hurting and guarded due to past experiences you have to deal with it. Or maybe you have just avoided dating because it all seems like too much to tackle. And there is never a right time. It isn't going to just go away, and you are sabotaging your own happiness by denying it.

Love is a need.

Many dating clients I have had over the years come to me specifically to learn how to date. However, I pick up very quickly that dating is not the issue. I can teach any women how to date and to have as many dates as she wants. That is not hard. What is hard is trying to get these women to deal with their dating fears and their mindsets that are sabotaging love. You cannot be guarded and vulnerable at the same time. Love requires you to put some skin in the game.

Time and time again, I meet women who are not dating or are not positioning themselves to meet men but then happen to meet a man randomly. In these instances, a few common things happen to damage the good girls. First, although guarded initially because she doesn't want to get hurt, she tends to allow this man to get too close too quickly because she is so starved for male attention and affection. Let's be honest, you are lonely and often times bored, which is very dangerous when you are single because you can fall prey to any man who shows interest. Once that wall comes down it comes down too fast, and you rush right in. He may have only said a few things you wanted to hear and you are practically half in love with him already. You haven't qualified or vetted him. You really don't even know him. He may or may not be ready for a relationship. It takes time to get to know people and determine their true intentions. We don't live in the 1950's were the social norms and rules dictated men be gentlemen and honorable. You cannot take these things for granted because now men get all the benefits of marriage from women without ever committing. This is the number one reason men say they don't feel pressured to get married…because they don't have to. They get sex, home-cooked meals, and emotional and spiritual support, everything that used to be reserved for marriage they now get freely from women to whom they haven't even committed.

Second, because you have moved too fast and have practically zero dating experience, you ignore or miss the red flags that this guy is a loser or user, especially if he has a polished or charming appearance and may fit your fairy tale image. You have been drinking the "good girl Kool-Aid" and trying to date like our mothers or grandmothers did by committing to the first half decent man you meet. You put all your eggs in one basket before you even know what you are committing to. You fall hook-line-and-sinker for the fantasy. Often even sleeping with this man because you think he is The One, your Boaz, your soulmate. By the time the smoke clears and you realize you've made a big mistake, you are emotionally connected with someone who doesn't love you or even has half the qualities you need in a husband. Or even if he is absolutely awesome, who cares? If he doesn't love you or is dating other women you are wasting your time. We cannot make a man ready for marriage. There is absolutely nothing you can do to make him commit.

Unfortunately, by this time, it is too late, now you are emotional, and it is hard to get over him. You could have found this out in the first month of dating if you knew how to date and go slow. With more experience, you could have dropped this zero after the third date without blinking an eye because you would have been going slow enough to feel God's little nudges and hear that small voice say, "He's not the One."

It is time for good girls to prepare for dating and meeting that special someone. Don't ignore your love life any longer. Consider investing in learning how to date and get positioned for love. Learn how to spot the losers and to take your time vetting and qualifying men for the purpose of marriage. I encourage you to do all these things so that you don't get hurt by the random men you do meet. God has a love story with your name on it. You are not meant to remain single.

> *God has a love story with your name on it.*

- Wounded Women -

This brings me to the third and final category of women who remain perpetually single, "Wounded Women." Women who are hurting are probably the largest category of women because there are plenty of alpha females and good girls who fall into this category as well. Women who are dealing with deep pain should not be dating. I will say it again, if you are deeply hurting, dealing with anxiety, have gone through great trauma, and have not gotten help to heal, YOU SHOULD NOT BE DATING. A man or relationship is not the answer to your problems or issues. A man is not going to make you happy. In most cases, relationships you get into while hurting only tend to bring more harm. This is because your choices in men when you are hurting are skewed. The pain of most women has come at the hands of a man, be it a father, stepfather, uncle, boyfriend, or husband.

> *A man or relationship is not the answer to your problems or issues.*

Many women have issues from absentee or abusive fathers, or rape and molestation from their childhoods. We women are so strong, and we just keep pushing through but the one area you can't hide your issues is in relationships. You can pursue your career, personal health, and wealth, but your pain shows when you try to relate to others because you must be able to trust and be vulnerable. This is where our past wounds and damage becomes evident. For this reason, many wounded women do not date at all. They may isolate themselves or avoid men that show interest.

In the last few years, I have done healing workshops for

women, and I'm always amazed by the high percentages of women who have been raped and molested, in their childhood or as an adult. In a workshop with twenty-five women, ninety-five percent of them have been abused in some way by a man. And most often it involves a man within the family structure breaking her trust as a child. We women don't tend to talk about these things. Many of my private healing clients have suffered great trauma, and I am often the first person they are telling about what happened. So many women are the walking wounded. To look at them, you would never know the pain behind their smiles. However, since relationships are the one area where you cannot hide, this pain will come out.

Many of these women also have self-esteem issues going back to a mentally or verbally abusive parent, ex-boyfriend, or ex-husband. We women are so sensitive to words, they literally hurt. We tend to internalize the words and incorporate them into our thinking causing us to feel ugly, fat, unworthy, or undeserving of love.

Low self-esteem is a major factor in how and why wounded women date and go into relationships. In truth, wounded women are looking for relief – relief from the pain, the toxic thinking and cycles of anxiety, or even depression. Hurting women often seek out love as temporary pain relief which most often comes in the form of sex. It is easy to meet men and fall into bed with them when you are hurting and seeking love and affection. I will go into greater detail on the risks of dating while damaged later. For now, understand that you cannot date while wounded. Wounded women are looking to be rescued and saved. And unkind men with bad intentions can see it a mile away. You become prey to men who are users and abusers. So I encourage you to heal first and then learn how to date.

- Get Real About Relationships -

Church doesn't teach us how to date. People quote Proverbs 31 constantly, but we don't live in those times. You are not Ruth. That is not your story. I met my husband through Facebook, one of my best friends met her soulmate on Bumble, and many of my clients meet their soulmates on Match.com or POF. Let that sink in girls. Everything has changed. You cannot afford to be dating "old fashioned." It is not an effective strategy. We have matching and coaching clients who struggle to find balance in this new world. It is fine if you are a traditional person who wants traditional gender roles, but you have to stick to it and only date men with the same values.

> *You cannot afford to be dating "old fashioned." It is not an effective strategy.*

If you want to be a stay-at-home mom, and your husband to be the financial breadwinner, you can't be Miss Independent. You are going to need to be very domesticated, and willing to allow the man to lead because the type of man you want is going to be looking for that in you. He doesn't mind being the provider and protector, but you have to take care of everything else including the house and kids.

If you are not traditional, you fall into seventy-four percent of the American population. This group either wants both parties to work or needs both parties to work, this includes women who are working or have entrepreneurial endeavors and men who want their wives to work and share the financial responsibilities. This paradigm shift requires us to adapt and, by that, I mean 21st Century relationships are *partnerships*. You are going to need to determine what you are good at and then determine what you need to help balance your life. When two people complement each other, a relationship can work like a great company. Two is always better than one, but first, you must plan and strategize for how your "company" is going to work. What roles and responsibilities will each person have? And this is no longer based on gender but instead based on capabilities, preferences, desires, skills, and passions. It is time to drop the fairy tale thinking of previous generations and get real about relationships.

Chapter 4 Reflections:

1. Which category of single women do you fit in?
2. Are you able to relate to all of the categories?
3. Identify three things about yourself that you can begin to work on to position yourself for love.
4. What are your strengths and weaknesses that you bring to a partnership?

5

THE SITUATIONSHIP SYNDROME

A Situationship is basically a pseudo-relationship, a placebo masking itself as a formative relationship. It smells like a relationship, it sort of looks like a relationship, and it may even feel like one, but it's not.[12]

A major side effect of dating difficulties and having true connections is people settle for a semblance of love and companionship. Many women I meet often admit they ignored signs that a man wasn't ready or they settled for less than God's best for their lives mostly because they were lonely or hopeful it could become better.

Many times we are also lazy about dating or even naive. We get ourselves in these situations because we don't vet these men before getting emotionally involved. We become comfortable with them over time. We are used to them, yet he is not your boyfriend or fiancé. There is no commitment, you don't use titles, and you aren't in a relationship – you are in a "situationship." Women are often in and out of these situationships whether

People aren't even dating anymore, just talking, catching feelings, sleeping together and ending up in a situationship.

they are aware of it or not. Some of them last years which really blurs the lines especially for women who feel these are real "relationships." And yes this is going on with women of faith (i.e., "Godly Girls") too. People aren't even dating anymore, just talking, catching feelings, sleeping together and ending up in a situationship.

There is a range of intimacy and levels to situationships that you need to be aware of as well. The men tell me all the time that the good girls or Christian girls are the worst. Although they claim to be "abstinent" initially, they are the first ones to initiate sex early on in dating. I will talk more about this later. However, it is understandable why men don't respect women or take their abstinence seriously because women don't stick to it when our resolve is tested. It is easy to be abstinent when you aren't dating or dating someone you don't like. But start dating someone who you are super attracted to, and it becomes much harder.

Many women who say they are abstinent are really more on a "sex sabbatical." These are the women who tend to say they are abstinent but quickly have sex when they meet someone they really like. It was never a deeper spiritual commitment centered on God, growth, purpose, and maturity. Before you lead with telling a man you are abstinent, be sure it is what you truly mean. It doesn't help women who are truly committed to abstinence to meet men who don't believe them or take them seriously.

When I met Mr. Pope, it was very difficult, and he is a pastor! We limped our way to the altar. We were in love, and a simple kiss ignited fireworks, especially the longer we went on dating and courting. The love continued to grow and magnify. So I am going to keep it very real about sex in this book. I am going to talk about what is really going on out here. Not how we want it to be or how it is supposed to be or how we wish it could be, but how it is!

Over the years I have made some interesting observations about the standards by which men and women are using to look for a partner. You notice that I say, men and women because no one is exempt. The casualness of dating and resulting situationships has taken a psychological toll on single people today. It's become so obvious that I have given it a name, the "Situationship Syndrome." Here are a few of my own personal stories, as well as common situations with clients. These stories illustrate my journey with this syndrome so you get a clear picture of what a situationship is and how it may be affecting your mindset about dating, compatibility, and your standards.

- Mr. Gorgeous -

Right after my divorce, and having zero dating experience, I met this very handsome man online, and we began having phone conversations frequently. Handsome doesn't really do him justice ladies, he was fine! He was 6'5", smooth chocolate complexion, a brilliant white smile, and a lean muscular physique. He looked like a model and was the most gorgeous man that I had ever met. For the sake of this story, we are going to call him Mr. Gorgeous. He was a struggling artist, pursuing a career in acting, and was a little bit younger than me. Situationships tend to be rooted in lust. Hence they are typically with men you find very attractive on some level, who often don't meet other relationship requirements.

Situationships tend to be rooted in lust. Hence they are typically with men you find very attractive on some level, who often don't meet other relationship requirements.

We began talking more and more over several months but, because he lived out of state, we didn't meet right away. Eventually, he was coming to my city, and we made a date to meet. I was already "in lust" before we even met, so it was no surprise that, after months of conversation, we practically slept together that first night. We didn't, but it was close girls. And remember this is the judgment free zone so before you throw me under the bus, I hope you can learn something from my mistakes.

This would begin an on and off again situationship that lasted many years. He always said all the right things. He made me feel so beautiful like I was the most beautiful woman in the world to him. And early on, he never said he didn't want a relationship…but I didn't ask either. I assumed we wanted the same things because I was so naïve and inexperienced. Initially, he said he wasn't a big kisser which is why he didn't want to kiss a lot. If a man tells you this he is a big fat liar, he is just not that into you, or he is trying to not get emotionally involved with you. Whenever he came to town, we would hang out, sleep together, and have fun.

Then he moved to my city, and we began seeing each other even more. I caught feelings. It began to feel like we were "something." Sex became more like love-making. The kissing became more passionate. He began to catch feelings too. We talked about trying to really be together. He said all the right things, yet his finances and lack of stability were always a great excuse as to why he wasn't ready. "He was pursuing his dreams, he wasn't raised to have a woman take care of him." All the right words that made him even more endearing.

He also came from a great, close-knit, church-going family and he adored his mother. All the things we look for in a relationship-ready man. The only problem is he wasn't relationship-ready.

But it sure felt like it. He even had a nickname for me that no one else used. I met his friends, they knew me by name yet we were not a couple. We ended up having a huge falling out because I found out he was sleeping with another girl and using her for her money, car, and house to crash when he was between gigs. Mind you, we were not "together," so I had no right to be upset however I was very hurt. We went for about a year not really talking. I met someone else, and it evolved into a relationship. That relationship eventually ended, and Mr. Gorgeous and I began talking and eventually sleeping together again. This went off and on for a long time. What hooked me about him were the following three things: he was gorgeous and always made me feel beautiful, we laughed constantly, and we had great sex. And being with him between serious relationships kept my "partner count" low. It didn't make me feel like I was promiscuous because I would even convince myself that we could potentially be together long-term. In truth, Mr. Gorgeous was essentially a very good looking maintenance man.

As a result of this situationship, here are some problems that developed in my mindset and how it sabotaged my dating experiences. Problem number one, most men do not look like Mr. Gorgeous. Less than two percent of the entire male population in the United States is over 6'4". Only four percent are over 6'2". And less than fifteen percent of men in the United States are 6'0" and taller. And that is just when you consider height, not race, or other physical attributes. When you add in his build, complexion, chiseled good looks, six-pack abs, and perfect smile, I estimate he is significantly less than one percent of the entire male population. Which means the likelihood that I was going to meet a man that looked like Mr. Gorgeous who was husband-material and marriage-minded, financially secure, and was mutually interested in me is slim to none. No man could physically compare to Mr. Gorgeous.

Problem number two, the "honeymoon" effect of this fun relationship made it very hard for other men to compete. Because we only saw each other infrequently, it was always fresh, new, and fun. That's not how real relationships are. However, the "fun factor" is very addictive. It will make you feel like other men are boring. He and I were never around each other long enough to deal with the daily, mundane workings of a real relationship. We didn't have bills, children, or a mortgage. All we had was chemistry and fun, not reality.

Which leads to problem number three, the no-strings-attached passionate sex that simulated "love-making." Having sex with someone who you are extremely attracted to can be very alluring. I relate this to being with a gorgeous celebrity. Average humans don't look like this. The lust factor only heightened the sexual experience. Nothing about this situationship was real. However, it set me up to compare every man I met to this false standard of love.

This is the Situationship Syndrome. Comparing real people and relationships to these pseudo-relationships is neither fair nor healthy, and it will leave you single for a very long time. Throughout all the on and off again years of dealing with Mr. Gorgeous, he was never my boyfriend, my man, or my fiancé. I was literally dating out of my league and beneath me, all at the same time. He was out of my league physically. He tended to be in relationships with little hard body fitness models. I was the beautiful, older, thicker, divorcee, mother of three, with ex-husband drama. And he was beneath me intellectually and spiritually. Just because a man will sleep with you and accept what

He desired me, he didn't value me. There's a difference.

you offer doesn't mean he sees you as a potential wife. He desired me, he didn't value me. There's a difference.

- The Baller -

My next story involves a man who I thought had it all. He wasn't as fine as Mr. Gorgeous, but he was tall, good-looking, and wealthy. He played professional ball for some years and was retired. He also had great relationships with his family and went to church with his mother regularly. We began talking and dating, and he began laying it on pretty thick. He wined and dined me. He had multiple luxury cars and homes. I would meet him in other states at one of his houses to spend long weekends. Money was not an issue whatsoever. I had my own money too, but his lifestyle was pretty lavish. At this point in my single life, I was really tired of dating and wanted a committed relationship that was leading to marriage.

I would initiate conversations with him to see where his head was and to gauge how ready he was for a relationship, see I was getting smarter girls! I was not satisfied with his answers. My feelings lessened as I began realizing he was a lot of fluff without much substance. It took me a minute to figure it out because of the "shiny ball' effect. All of the flashy cars and houses, flights, dinners, and shopping had been so much fun that I lost focus on the things that really mattered to me. I also quickly discovered I wasn't the only woman he was doing all of this with. When I began asking really direct questions, I realized I wasn't in a relationship at all. This was another situationship that just seemed like a relationship. If you never have the commitment conversation, he isn't your boyfriend. Period.

After I broke it off with him and notice I say it like we were "breaking up," but if you were never officially together you technically can't break up. I point this out because, as a relationship coach and matchmaker, women often give me their relationship history with their "exes" yet after more digging it's apparent they have had a string of situationships – not actual relationships. He was never your boyfriend or "your man" so he isn't your ex. And is it any wonder we get so hurt and damaged by these pseudo-relationships? After all, we aren't built for this type of thing.

So I stopped seeing Mr. Baller…much to his surprise. These types of men are not used to women breaking it off with them. He was literally in shock. Of course, this made him want me even more, but I was firm. I knew he wasn't the one for me and I didn't want to just play house. I wanted the real thing. I wanted love, and I was tired of wasting time with men who weren't getting me to my goals.

- The Nice Guy -

Something really interesting happened after dating Mr. Baller. I met this man who was an engineer and professor. A very nice man. A good man. He was husband material. I agreed to a date, he picks me up, we go to dinner and have a perfectly pleasant time. Afterward, I called one of my best friends to tell him about the date.

My friend could tell I wasn't very excited about this guy. So he asked me what was wrong, and I said, "He is a nice guy, but he drives a Ford Explorer." My friend got so upset with me. He called me out on it and said: "You've never talked like that before, that's not who you are, you aren't materialistic like that." I stopped and really thought about it and realized he was right. That is not me. What the heck had happened to me?

Just from dating Mr. Baller for a short period of time, my financial and materialistic expectations skyrocketed. I somehow felt the Ford Explorer guy wasn't good enough or I could do better. I felt entitled. Imagine if I hadn't had a really good friend to bring me back to Earth. Imagine if I had been corrupted by this experience and incorporated these financial requirements into my long-term standards for relationship compatibility. Are you beginning to see how situationships and false standards can sabotage your chances for true love? These situations are not real, so it is totally ridiculous to compare real, commitment-minded men to these men who just wanted to play.

- Secret Lover/Side-Chick -

The next scenario is one I haven't personally experienced but one I frequently see with women I've coached and matched. Many find themselves in short or long-term situations with men they actually considered a real relationship. They are sleeping with these men, cooking for them, and doing everything women do in committed relationships; however, they ignore the fact that, although you may have met some of his family or close friends, he always disappears when it matters most. He rarely, if ever, takes you out in public. You are always at your house. He comes over to visit at all types of crazy hours, yet you never go to his house. Or, if he has money, you may go to hotels or an apartment he keeps, but there's a house you don't know about. He doesn't always answer the phone when you call or respond to text messages right away. And he always has great excuses. But as soon as he comes over again, all is forgiven, and you keep seeing him.

You are the side-chick without even realizing it. He either has a girlfriend or a wife, and you are the only one who doesn't know it. These types of men are very good at playing these games. They are so good, in fact, that it is hard for you to realize you're a side-chick because of how often you see him. Even the friends and family are in on it. They keep his secrets. By the time you discover he is married or in a relationship, you are so emotionally involved that it's very difficult to disengage and resist him. This happens to the best of women, women who swore they would never date a married man.

The side-chick scenario may be one of the most psychologically damaging situationships because it affects your self-esteem and self-worth. Women often find themselves continuing the cycle of dating emotionally unavailable men because, deep down, they don't feel worthy. They begin to settle for just having "somebody" or "anybody" to not be alone or to avoid being vulnerable. If he is married, then you know that you can't get hurt because he is unavailable. These situationships have caused so much damage that some women find it hard to have healthy standards for love and marriage. They continue to make bad decisions in men, only adding insult to injury. Unfortunately, when a good man comes along who truly wants to love her, she has difficulty receiving and accepting the love.

When a good man comes along who truly wants to love her, she has difficulty receiving and accepting the love.

These are just a few of the scenarios that cause the Situationship Syndrome in modern dating. And men have it too. These examples are from a female perspective, but men deal with the syndrome's fallout as well. Men want to be loved just like women do, for who they are and not for what they have. Men deal with "Gold Digger" situationships, "Serial Dater" situationships, "I'm Just Bored" situationships, and so on. They are very concerned about being used but, in the meantime, these situationships create false standards around beauty and sex that have nothing to do with finding a wife or real love.

Situationships have both men and women so warped that their requirements are sabotaging their opportunities for true love. You may say things to yourself like "I'm not picky, I refuse to settle." Your friends may often tell you that you are picky and you just don't believe them. Most of your friends are married, and you are holding out for this "unicorn man" because, in your mind, you have a created a "Build-a-Bear" mentality. You are taking pieces and parts from each man you have experienced and have constructed the perfect man in your imagination. And because you have experienced these attributes previously, it doesn't seem far-fetched to you. When, in actuality, it isn't realistic that one man can embody what it took five different men to give you.

It isn't realistic that one man can embody what it took five different men to give you.

These are all things to consider. Have your previous choices and situations shaped your desires and expectations? This is something to think about seriously as you get ready for love and marriage.

Chapter 5 Reflections:

1. Have you been in a situationship? Or in love with a man that didn't love you?
2. How has it affected you?
3. Have you incorporated situationship thinking into your requirements for true love?
4. Do you claim exes that never committed to you and subconsciously compare new men to them?

6

DATING WHILE DAMAGED

Women and men come to my agency seeking answers and help. People are hurting. Men and women. Life has a way of taking its toll on all of us. And none of us are exempt. Men are often hurting because they internalize everything and do not feel able to verbalize their trapped emotions without being judged as "not being a real man." Women come to us often in denial. They want love and marriage, which initiates them working with us, but we quickly assess that healing and a new mindset are the biggest needs. I too have walked a path of pain…

After a very messy and painful divorce from my second husband, I found myself single for the first time in my adult life. I was hurting over two failed marriages, and my children were hurting over this most recent divorce. I was bruised, broken, and also in denial about how damaged I was both emotionally and spiritually. I had done what my parents said to do. I had married instead of having sex outside of marriage. I had worked hard and built a financially secure life. I had tried so hard to make the "right" choices that I ended up in a marriage where I was miserable. I was desperate to make different choices to not repeat history. I was truly afraid of failure.

The divorce cleaned me out financially. I lost everything. My rental property, my savings, my 401K, my credit, all gone. So, like many people, I began to seek God due to great pain, heartache, and distress. However, as soon as I would get back on top of most aspects of my life, I would stop surrendering to God and go back to my own agenda. Shortly after that, I was back on hard times again. I wrestled with God for control of my life. I had my own plan, and He had His. I am one of those people who struggle with trying to do everything in my own strength. I try to make things happen through sheer will and determination. I can be very stubborn and a control freak. This vicious cycle of surrendering and then reclaiming personal control went on for many years. Not long after my divorce, I began pursuing one of my dreams to start a construction company. Over the next several years my company began getting more and more business. It eventually broke more than a million dollars in sales! Through a series of other ventures, I found myself coaching, motivating, and matching people as well. I was doing it part-time, but things built momentum. In retrospect, I had backed my way into my purpose – one talent, one business, and one opportunity at a time. Each choice led to the next level of purpose and passion. It felt like I stumbled upon it.

> *I began to seek God due to great pain, heartache, and distress.*

I started becoming well known for helping people get unstuck and heal from their dating challenges and then matching them with their new love. I always wanted to help people full time, so it seemed like God was bringing things full circle. Success was growing, and I even had a savings account again! I had a radio show every Saturday in Atlanta where we talked about love, relationships, sex, dating, and marriage. I loved it. I began speaking at conferences and was matching people with great success. The first couple I ever matched got married, I was hooked.

Although I was helping other people find success in love, the irony was not lost on me that I was still single and continued making the same wrong choices in men. My type had remained the same since I got divorced: cute, fun, crazy about me, businessman, making nothing less than six figures. Needless to say, I was meeting some really great men. However, I knew each one wasn't The One in my heart.

It was okay though. I was super busy! I loved my life again! ...Or so I tried to tell myself. I was helping other people heal and connect, so it was almost as if it was happening to me. Except it wasn't. Underneath, I was unhappy because it wasn't the abundant life I desired and knew I deserved.

I was still hurting. I was scared and afraid of failure. I was ashamed of my choices. I felt alone. Success without love is very empty. The stress levels over the years had taken their toll. I would have a glass of wine or two before going on air for the radio show. I told myself it was just to calm my nerves. I would drink too much at events and told myself that everyone is having a good time, why shouldn't I have some fun too? I was coping, holding on to control by a very thin thread. I stayed busy just so I wouldn't have to deal with my fears. I was running. Running from God and running from myself. I was dating and discarding men left and right and probably hurt some in the process.

> *Success without love is very empty.*

And then everything fell apart right when it all was seemingly coming together. My mother died. She had fought cancer for ten years, and it had returned again with a vengeance. Within five weeks of being told the cancer had spread…my mom was gone. I was with her those last few days. I was with her when she took her last breath. There are no words to describe this loss for me. Grief engulfed me like a cloud. She was my rock. My biggest fan and cheerleader. She told me every day when I was growing up that I could do and be anything I put my mind to. When all was lost, she was the one person who always had words of wisdom and support.

I know everyone loves their mothers; however, I truly had a great one who connected me to loving people and seeing the best in them. I am the product of her unconditional love, wit, humor, and strength and my father's heart for people and ministry. To everyone on the outside, I was holding it all together so well. After all, I have three sons, and my father came to live with me as well after my mom passed. I had too much on my plate to lose my mind or fall apart. I could not lose it! Or could I?

Unknowingly, my parents had allowed their insurance to lapse. As their only child, the bulk of the financial responsibility for my mother's arrangements fell to me as did the care for my father afterward. I watched as $20,000 in savings began going out the door. Within two months, it was gone. By the third month, I couldn't pay my rent. By the fifth month, I was being evicted. My mother's death had left me numb. I wasn't working, I wasn't focused. I was scared out of mind as the money dwindled. Yes, there was family I could ask for help. It didn't even cross my mind. I asked people who I thought would be there for me, includ-

> *I couldn't take anymore. I was falling apart.*

ing the man I was dating. He disappeared. It is amazing how much you learn about people when you need help. It really shows you who is in your corner. I already had so much stress and pain that I hadn't dealt with my mother's death being the last straw. I couldn't take anymore. I was falling apart.

I was so used to God providing for me, even up to the last minute, I never imagined I would actually be evicted. This was twice that I had lost nearly everything. First with the divorce and now this. I was so broken and confused. Through all the years of struggling to get my businesses off the ground, I never had anything like this happen. I didn't understand what God was doing. Why? Why now? Why like this? And then, within two weeks of being evicted, my construction company got the largest order we had ever had. That was even more confusing. Only two weeks earlier and I wouldn't have been evicted!

I was emotionally broken. My mother is gone, He could have healed her, why didn't He? God and I had to do a lot of talking. I was so hurt and scared. All I had was my car, my sons, and my best friend, Simone. She said all great people have these kinds of stories. You are the next Oprah! You learn who loves you during these types of times. Soon after my mother's death, my Dad came to live with me full time. He was dying a slow death without my mother. They had been together forty-two years. He needed his family to heal.

So again, just like after my divorce, I had to start rebuilding. This time, I was so shattered that my prayers began to change. I just started asking God for His will to be done in my life. Obviously, I didn't know what the heck I was doing so I didn't trust myself anymore. And there was a new fear that had taken root in me, a fear of lack. I was so anxious and afraid of losing everything again. I was exhausted from trying and trying. I began to lay everything at God's feet because all of this was just too much. It is through our broken places that we learn who we are and our purpose. And it is through these experiences that I truly surrendered to God and discovered and accepted His true purpose for my life.

It is through our broken places that we learn who we are and our purpose.

It's from this place that I stopped relying on alcohol, work, and men to cope. It is from here that I launched the coaching and matchmaking agency. It is from this place that I met the man God had promised me, my soulmate, and the greatest love of my life. It is from this place that I became healed. It is from this place that I began to walk in my own truth of who I am and why I am here on this Earth. It is from this place that my life was forever changed.

You may be reading this chapter and thinking you are okay. After all, you don't have any major issues, or you've moved on successfully after the pain. However, if you are struggling with love, dating, or relationships, I ask that you take a moment to answer these simple questions as an assessment of whether you may have toxic emotional baggage:

1. Have you been through a traumatic or systematic experience such as abuse of any kind? Mental, verbal, emotional, sexual, or physical? As an adult or as a child? This could be a verbally abusive parent, a manipulative ex-husband or boyfriend, or possibly rape or molestation?
2. Do you have abandonment issues stemming from the death of a loved one or parent? Or an absentee parent?

3. Have you been through a bad relationship or divorce that left you heartbroken? Or a series of bad or damaging relationships?
4. Have you internalized negative words and opinions of others and made them your own?
5. Have you ever sought help such as counseling or therapy to help you overcome any of these issues mentioned above?

There are a hundred of other possibilities, situations, or circumstances that may have caused damage. I have just named a few of the most common causes that I see with clients. If you have not gotten any help working through painful issues from your past, it is very likely you have some toxic emotional baggage. Allow me to explain. As women, we have a tendency to act as if we are always okay. We "take a lickin' and keep on tickin'." We are survivors. So many women I meet are hurting so deeply yet, to look at them, you would never know that behind the pretty smiles and confident appearance is a wounded soul. We often hide very deep pain, even from ourselves. And, as I have mentioned, it is in relationships that we can't fake it. If you have low self-esteem, are insecure, afraid, or angry, it is going to come out in either the inability to have a healthy relationship, or you are going to avoid deep commitments to prevent the possibility of further pain.

Behind the pretty smiles and confident appearance is a wounded soul.

If this is you, I highly recommend you reach out to my agency for our Healed to Love course to work with one of our therapist or counselors. There are gifted people who have made it their life's work to help you heal. And it isn't as hard as you may think. It starts with first admitting you need help. Once you open up and stop denying that some things are holding you back, it is amazing how quickly the healing process can proceed. It is a choice – a choice that you want to be happy and free from the burden of pain. It is a choice to forgive yourself and others, not because they always deserve it, but because you know forgiveness will free you. It is for you, your happiness and your beautiful smile, it is not for them. It is between you and God.

Healing and living whole is so necessary to attracting and keeping love. And we are not going to make this complicated because it's not. It is a choice. It is a choice that you are going to make every day, one day at a time. And this is your personal responsibility. It is not the responsibility of your future partner to work on your issues. No matter how deep or old your wounds are, it is necessary for you to start uncovering them and healing today. No more acting like everything is okay. "I was raped, but I am okay." "I was abused, but I am okay." "I have never talked about it, but I am okay." "I have trust issues, but I am okay." No one is perfect, but you have to be on the path to healing and wholeness. You have to stop denying there is a problem.

Have you ever noticed the person who is hurting the most in a relationship gets all the attention? The energy of the relationship is therefore always focused on that person's feelings, drama, and unhappiness. They are energy vampires! As a couple, you can't even focus on just enjoying the relationship because half of the relationship is broken. If you want a happy and healthy relationship, *be* a happy and healthy person first. I am going to lay out some very practical steps for how to begin healing and letting go of your past.

This is a process you will continue to work on throughout your time being single and even once you are with the love of your life. Some hurts are deeper than others, but you can choose today to stop allowing these things to block you from receiving the love you deserve.

If you want a happy and healthy relationship, be a happy and healthy person first.

At the heart of all your relationships is YOU. How you relate to yourself – your self-image, self-esteem, self-talk – lays the foundation for every relationship you build. If you doubt yourself, others will too. If you find yourself hard to love, so will others. One of the most important things you can do to prepare for love and marriage is to stop ignoring your issues and get the healing you need. In today's world, people have a lot less patience to deal with your problems. It isn't their job to heal you or make you happy. Happiness is an inside job. And it is kind of a catch twenty-two because, if you are "dating while damaged," you will attract damaged people or people who only damage you more.

You will meet people that keep adding insult to injury because you will both find each other relatable because of your common pain. Or you become easy prey to men who don't have good intentions. There is nothing worse than messy matches. Your own mess matches their mess, so you feel like it is love. These relationships are a train wreck waiting to happen. Maybe you have been in one or have a friend who always finds herself in these situations. The common denominator is the damaged individual who keeps moving from relationship to relationship looking for a different result. And just like "driving while drunk" can lead to serious injury, "dating while damaged" can derail your life and leave you feeling hopeless about love.

So where does the healing start so love can result? My first principle of love is love starts with you.

- Self-Love -

What is Self-Love? It seems like this term is thrown around so much now. "Love yourself first, to attract love." I say it all of the time but what does this really mean? How do we practice this in our everyday life? How do we change bad habits, so we begin treating ourselves the same way we expect others to love, trust, and respect us?

My first principle of love is love starts with you.

As I said, my first principle of love is learning to love yourself to create a life that is happy, peaceful, fulfilling and attracts the love you desire. Loving yourself often means taking a break from dating and taking time for reflection. Many people feel they have taken the necessary time to heal because they haven't dated for a while. Even if you haven't been dating, it doesn't mean you are healed. It just means you took a break from dating. There is a huge difference between taking a break and actually taking the time to work on becoming a better version of yourself.

Mv best advice to ready yourself for dating is…stop dating.

My best advice to ready yourself for dating is... stop dating.

If you are sexually active with someone, stop immediately. From here we are going to work together to build your happy life, one step at a time. In a practical way, you are going to learn what makes you happy, so you hold others to those standards. Remember, in dating, you want additions, not subtractions. So if you are full of joy, peace, and love when you meet someone, and he then causes you stress and unhappiness, it is very easy to see he isn't enhancing and adding to your life, he is subtracting. Adios muchacho!

So let's start by defining self-love as it pertains to the process in this book and how it plays out in you attracting your soulmate. Self-love[13] is:

1. Regard for one's own well-being and happiness, chiefly considered as a desirable rather than narcissistic characteristic, so it's not selfishness, rather self-interest.
2. It is a state of appreciation for oneself that grows from actions that support our physical, psychological, and spiritual growth.
3. It grows by actions that mature us. Through it, we begin to understand our weaknesses as well as our strengths.
4. It causes us to have more compassion for ourselves as human beings struggling to find personal meaning, more centered in our life purpose and values, and expect living fulfillment through our efforts.

The way I best describe Self-Love is beginning to live very honestly. Honest about who you are, what you want, your thoughts, actions, and intentions. It is removing the layers of self-doubt and the expectations others place on you. It is moving from a position of fear to a position of faith. It is the beginning of living your life fulfilled and happy, separate and apart from what others think and expect of you. It's asking for what you want, so you get what you desire from God and others. It is the most authentic and real version of yourself. If you are unwilling, to be honest with yourself and don't know who you are and where you are going, how can you make choices and have intentions to bring about God's best in your life?

We have a tendency to pretend we are happy when we aren't. We do what we think is the right thing instead of speaking our true thoughts and feelings. We worry about what others think of us. In other words, we are in prisons that we have created – mental and spiritual prisons of our own making. We live afraid. Afraid of repeating our mistakes. Afraid of failure and lack. Most of our motivations come from fear and shame. Even half of the things you think you need and want in a future spouse are based on your fears of repeating the past. Our thinking is flawed. You believe wrong. You think wrong. Therefore you speak wrong and act wrong. You don't truly believe in God's best for you. Your predominant thoughts are negative, shameful, doubtful, and critical. You aren't nice to yourself, yet when others treat you this way you are highly upset, hurt, and offended.

So let's start with the Bible's definition of Love and apply it to ourselves first:

> "Love is patient, love is kind, it does not envy, it does not boast, it is not proud. It does not dishonor others, it is not self-seeking, it is not easily angered, it keeps no record of wrongs. Love does not delight in evil but rejoices with the truth. It always protects, always trusts, always hopes, always perseveres."
>
> 1 Cor. 13: 4-8 New Living Translation

Read this verse several times. If you can't practice loving yourself like this then how can you possibly try to love another on this level? Let's be clear, this verse describes true love, godly love. This is the type of unconditional love and acceptance we want in our soulmate. This is the love I found for the first time in my life, after two marriages and three sons. After meeting Kerry, I realized I had never truly loved another person before. He is my soulmate.

So let's examine the verse. "Love is patient, love is kind, it does not envy, it does not boast, it is not proud." Are you patient with yourself? Are you kind to yourself? Are your predominant thoughts full of good and happy things for yourself? Do you truly believe your future is bright and promised? Or do you beat yourself up constantly, reminding yourself of your mistakes, questioning and doubting each decision in life, motivated by fears? Do you envy others? Comparing yourself with those around you? Looking at social media and wondering why is my life so hard when it seems so great for others? Are you proud and boastful when things are good only to fall into despair when things don't turn out the way you think they should?

Do you truly believe your future is bright and promised?

"It does not dishonor others, it is not self-seeking, it is not easily angered, it keeps no record of wrongs." Are you selfish? Always looking out for yourself and not treating others how you desire to be treated? Every relationship in your life is a testament to your relationship with God and yourself. How you treat others is truly how you feel about yourself. Are you angry? Do you take hurt out on others, instead of looking inward? If so, I encourage you to look at yourself and upward to heal and forgive yourself so you can love freely. Are you constantly keeping a record of your wrongs? Are your thoughts critical and judgmental? Do you always put yourself down for your mistakes? That's not loving.

"Love does not delight in evil but rejoices with the truth. It always protects, always trusts, always hopes, and always perseveres." Delight yourself in the truth of who you are, where you are, and what you have come through. You have persevered. Do not be ashamed. Loving yourself starts with knowing you have a God who will always protect and you can always trust, always hope. And God's love is the same love that is in you. You must simply remind yourself constantly of the divine spirit inside of you, and of who you are and what you are capable of accomplishing. It starts with loving yourself and everyone around you.

All of this sounds great right but *how* do you do this? Often books, church, and advice fall short of examples and practical application. I don't want that for you, so I've provided six steps – which are most effective when they become habits – for changing your thoughts and actions to live a life full of love, peace, and joy.

- Step 1: Pray -

Begin talking to God about everything that is going on. All your fears, concerns, problems, anxiety, shame, guilt, and remorse. Ask for forgiveness when necessary. Forgive yourself for your part in things or situations that still haunt you or things you have buried. Imagine when you pray that you are laying all of these things at God's feet. Tell Him that this is all just too much for you, so you're relinquishing it.

Ask God to help you heal. Ask Him to guide you to the people, books, and knowledge you need to truly heal. And when He begins to make these connections, do not ignore them. That counseling service that keeps popping up in your Facebook timeline, that referral from a friend who got amazing results with a life coach, that book everyone is talking about that you haven't read. God brings help and is always answering our prayers. Recognize the signs and answers He is giving but, first, you must ask. This requires you to stop denying that you even need help. Healing requires you get honest about your pain. Research shows that ninety percent of our pain in life is due to trapped emotions. The toxic baggage you may be carrying is not only sabotaging your love life, but it also affects your money, your health, your purpose. It is hurting every area of your life. Did you know sixty-one percent of cancer patients have deep issues of unforgiveness?14 You cannot afford to ignore your emotional and spiritual pain.

- Step 2: Meditate -

Prayer is talking to God. Meditation is listening. Take time to be quiet every day. Learn to sit still and silence your mind. This is so necessary to begin developing the discipline of being aligned and connected with God. It has been used for thousands of years to remove anxiety and fear from daily life and increase healing, peace, health, and mindfulness. If this seems hard at first, that is okay, don't stop. Challenge yourself to start with just five minutes a day. There are several apps and tools you can use to help you with this new habit. Wake up and do this in the morning before you start your day. This takes discipline. I advise my clients to set the alarm on their phone, so they have a daily reminder. Do not skip days. If you forget to do it in the morning, take five minutes in your car or on your lunch break. You can do this anywhere and at any time.

> *It is in this sacred place of peace that you can hear and listen to God in a whole new way.*

The important thing is to do it every day because it's what we do consistently that brings about long-term change in our lives. And over time, you are going to start feeling and being guided by God. You may hear a small, quiet voice inside of you. This can sometimes be a thought, a nudge, a feeling you should do something. A solution. An answer. It is in this sacred place of peace that you can hear and listen to God in a whole new way. You will learn to run to this place for joy, balance, love, and insight.

- Step 3: Practice Thanksgiving and Gratitude -

Begin to develop an attitude of gratitude. Thank God for all your blessings. Thank Him for life, protection, health, wealth, your family, and your friends – everything you can be thankful for. Sometimes you may only be able to be thankful for waking up that morning and breathing. That's okay. Whatever you can be grateful for, give thanks. This will position you to receive so much more. Gratitude will begin to unlock your abundant life. You want gratitude to become your default. If you learn how to be grateful even in difficult times, things will begin to turn around. We bring about what we think about so center your thoughts and feelings on love, thankfulness, and good things.

> *Develop an attitude of gratitude.*

- Step 4: Affirmations -

Does practicing prayer, meditation, and gratitude mean you will have completely positive thoughts throughout the day? No. You are going to have to reprogram your mind to think like God.

> "Finally, brothers and sisters, whatever is true, whatever is noble, whatever is right, whatever is pure, whatever is lovely, whatever is admirable – if anything is excellent or praiseworthy – think about such things"
>
> Phil 4:8 New International Version

The best way to do this is with affirmations. Affirmations are words or phrases you recite throughout your day to remind you of who you are, where you are going, and the beautiful future ahead of you. Here are some practical examples of affirmations and techniques to affirm self-love.

Our thoughts control our feelings, and our feelings control our actions.

The Etch-a-Sketch Technique. Daily we often see and hear things that can cause fear, doubt, and melancholy. Remember, our thoughts control our feelings, and our feelings control our actions. Instead of letting that thought continue, immediately shake your head back and forth, like an Etch-a-Sketch, and erase that negative thought and feeling. Then replace it with one of your affirmations. A favorite affirmation of mine is "I am so blessed! Everything I touch is blessed!"

Humor/Laughing. Personally, laughter always makes me feel better. If I can lighten my mood, I will immediately shift back into my Self-Love mode. Back to those pure and perfectly good thoughts. Come back to the present, and where you are now because you are not who you used to be. You have grown, learned, and become better.

Google "Affirmations." Write some down you really like and make you feel good. Start practicing saying them and use the Etch-a-Sketch method to replace negative thoughts with positive thoughts. You can also use your favorite scriptures as affirmations. "I am the head and not the tail" for example.

- Step 5: Visualization -

You need to practice having happy thoughts and images in your head. This is the whole idea behind Vision Boards. I have my clients create virtual vision boards. On your phone, create a folder in your images app and name it "My Happy Life." Download pictures of all your desires, goals, and interests. Anything that makes you feel good. Make sure there is a picture of a happy couple in there so you can imagine you and your soulmate enjoying life together. Look at this album every day. Before you know it, you will have real pictures of your real life to add to the collection.

- Step 6: The Happy List -

As I recommended, you need to take a break from dating and focus on healing and self-love. What are you going to do with all of your time since aren't dating? You are going to focus on you! And all the things that make you happy. Create a "happy list" of twenty things that make you smile, feel good, and even new interests or hobbies you've always wanted to try but always put off for the future. Now is the time to do these things. This is your life, and it is time to start living. Some of my own examples are taking a cooking class, riding my bike, bowling with friends, joining a book club, and relaxing with candles and bubble baths. List out everything you can think of besides dating. These things are not dependent on the opposite sex to bring you joy. This is all about you.

Now, you may struggle to come up with twenty, which means you really haven't been focusing on yourself enough. This should be easy. If not, keep adding to the list as you continue to brainstorm.

Happy Homework. For the first 30 days of focusing on yourself, you need to do three to four things off your list every week to make you happy. This will help you form the new habit of making yourself happy through daily activities. You are essentially dating yourself, learning to enjoy life on your own as an individual before God brings your soulmate. This is essential in attracting love. Everybody loves happy people. A smile is universally attractive. Start living your best life now, and you are on the path to your true love. This will also become a great place spiritually to start dating from again. You are happy, whole, loving your life not looking for anything except the one that enhances this experience. You are so at peace and loving life that you would rather be at home enjoying a good movie than to accept a date with someone that you aren't truly interested in. You are comfortable in your own skin. This helps you to be patient while waiting on your soulmate to arrive.

Start living your best life now, and you are on the path to your true love.

Chapter 6 Reflections:

1. As you examine your life and experiences, do you currently have damage and pain that needs to be addressed?
2. If so, what intentional actions are you going to take to get healed?
3. As it pertains to self-love, are you kind to yourself? Do you believe God's best for your life through your thoughts, words, and actions?
4. Challenge yourself to create daily habits that support self-love and personal well-being.

7

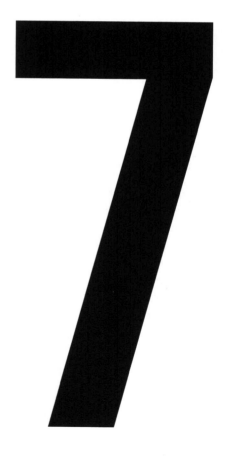

BLESSING BLOCKERS

You are the common denominator of every relationship you are in therefore the most likely cause of you remaining single is YOU. When I first became a matchmaker, before I met my own soulmate, I wasn't teaching the methods I share with you in this book because I hadn't experienced it for myself. So like many of my clients I thought, I just haven't met the right guy yet. Or maybe I am too fat, or my credit isn't good enough. These guys just want skinny, easy girls. They are intimidated by my success. I am so deep, they just don't understand me. Blah, blah, blah.

So, as a new matchmaker, I would listen to my clients' long list of requirements in a match, the whole time thinking, where am I going to find this person? This is isn't Build-a-Bear workshop! We aren't making men in a lab. Nevertheless, I would do my best to fulfill the clients' requests because I was dating with the same faulty thinking as my clients. I would try to match them with compatible men who met as much of the client's wish list as possible who were also marriage-minded. This became increasingly difficult because the men that fit the financial and physical requirements were not ready for commitment and vice versa the men who were ready weren't wealthy enough or good looking enough.

As matching would begin, it became obvious that we were looking for the proverbial needle-in-a-haystack. But a hired matchmaker should just be able to order up whatever the client wants in a mate, right? Wrong. This is still real life. Average men don't fit all of these requirements and whoever you like has to like you too. And someone can have eighty percent of what you think you want and need and it still isn't good enough. Why? Because our thinking is flawed when it comes to love and a match and I was guilty of it as well. Both my clients and I were blocking our blessings with our faulty thinking.As God began helping me correct my thinking and habits, I began coaching my clients through the same lessons. And, guess what, matching got easier. More people fell in love, and I met my soulmate. So I am going to give you my personal story of how I stopped blocking my blessings in the hopes you can learn from how I ultimately overcame my flawed thinking.

I got married very young and was married for ten years and had two sons with my second husband. We were two totally different people, and our primary struggles stemmed from a difference in spiritual depth, ambition, and financial goals. He was simpler in desires and creature comforts. I dreamed big. Always pushing and striving for more success. Truth be told, we were spiritually and purposefully incompatible. We did not share a common destiny. We made great friends but soulmates we were not.

> *Each consecutive relationship or dating experience, I would add a little more to my list based on my experiences of what didn't work.*

When we finally divorced, and I became single, on top of my original desires to be with a man that was handsome, fun, and loved me, I added additional requirements that he makes six-figures, be ambitious, and entrepreneurial in spirit. In other words, adding the things that I felt were missing in my marriage. And each consecutive relationship or dating experience, I would add a little more to my list based on my experiences of what didn't work. This included my situationship experiences as well. So by the time I was thirty-five to forty years old, my requirements had become absolutely ridiculous. Who can live up to these standards? Honestly, I wasn't even living up to these standards that I had for others. Nobody is perfect, not me and not my clients.

In addition to my list of growing requirements, I also inherited some thinking from my parents and my youth. My mother used to tell me that "you can do bad all by yourself" and two people don't need to be together struggling. This reinforced my six-figure successful man criteria for selecting men to date. As an adult, I now realize my mother just didn't want me to struggle financially as she and my father had. That brings me to my father. He was a pastor my entire life. He raised me with very strict rules around sex, marriage, and relationships which greatly influenced why I married so young. I was making my sex legal. I blamed my choices in marriage on this strict religious upbringing instead of taking responsibility for my own decisions. Needless to say, I didn't want anything to do with organized religion in my adult life. So the thought of marrying a pastor was an absolute deal breaker.

So let's summarize, I only dated, tall, handsome, fun men who were crazy about me, who made six-figures, were very ambitious and entrepreneurial, and who were definitely *not* pastors. That may sound reasonable to many of you. It was reasonable to me then. I didn't even feel like I was as picky as some people. And I always met great men. I primarily dated CEOs and alpha males with the occasional super good looking man thrown in for fun. However, despite their resumes and success, none of them were my soulmate. While I thought I had it all figured out, I didn't have a clue as to what I really needed to be happy and fulfilled. I just did not want to repeat the mistakes of my past. I was making decisions based on fear and shame, not love. Something had to change, I was becoming exhausted. Tired of dating. Tired of trying. Tired of being let down and disappointed again.

As I mentioned earlier, while doing all this dating, I was also in the middle of starting companies and starting to match and coach people. And then that breaking point came. I lost everything. My mother died. I lost my home. I didn't know what to do. Now, I don't believe you have to lose everything to surrender all to God. I just happen to be very stubborn, so my journey was slower and a little rougher. You can repeat these steps I learned and gain more quickly from my pain.

When I lost everything and felt like my life was being torn apart, I turned to God. And I quit dating and went through the healing process described in chapter six. And at this time, my prayers changed as well. I was desperate. I just couldn't take any more suffering. So I gave everything to God, I dropped my agenda. My agenda when it came to men, money, my companies, everything. In your case, it may just be your soulmate, but for me it was everything. I gave up every idea and thought about what I needed and wanted in a partner. If I had it right, wouldn't I have been married already? So I had to admit I had no idea what I was doing. And then I prayed these specific prayers:

1. I asked God for His will to be done in my life.
2. "God I give up. I put my desire for my soulmate in your hands. I can't do this without you. I surrender."

3. "I trust you, God, that whoever you have for me is perfect for me in every way. I trust you."

Simply put. I surrendered. What I didn't realize then is that by surrendering my will to God completely, it opened me up to receive my purpose and the greater meaning of my life. Remember what I said about self-love, that it is living the most authentic version of self. Therefore, living out your purpose is self-love to the highest degree, and it is also when you are closest to God because God is Love in all forms.

It is only when you start being real that real love shows up.

True love is about authenticity. It is about being your most true self and following your purpose path. It is only when you drop all the façade, pride, ego, and false expectations that you are led to your soulmate. It is only when you start being real that real love shows up. It is how I met Kerry.

- Settling versus Compromising -

There is a huge difference between settling and compromising. Settling is giving up on your needs. Compromising is understanding that no one is perfect and while your needs are being met, not all of your wants are being met. In dating, the difference between settling and compromising is very simple. The difference is love. Love is the one thing you can't afford to compromise. You can compromise on income, height, and personality, but you can't settle for anything less than love, friendship, respect, and trust. These are the key ingredients of a healthy relationship and marriage. Without them, you won't be fulfilled, and you won't be happy. Unfortunately, this is quite the opposite from how many people approach dating, they refuse to compromise on income, height, and a myriad of other requirements which completely edges out love.

I have worked with hundreds of women and men to help them stop the self-sabotaging behavior and blocking their own blessings. One major culprit that holds women and men back from true love is ego and fear. Ego and fear cause us to want a partner based on the perceptions of others, status, wealth, image, and even pressures from our family and friends.

I am going to give you several of the most common client profiles I have had over the years that were getting in their own way. Some of these women I have been able to help because they were truly ready and willing. And others I was not because they were not yet ready to surrender and change. Your results depend on your willingness to adapt, learn, and change. This point in life is different for everyone. For me, it was being emotionally and spiritually exhausted. For you, I pray it doesn't have to be so drastic. I believe you can make a choice today to start down a new path. As you read these descriptions think about yourself and if one of these mindsets may be your blessing blocker.

Puppy Love. My first client profile example is those who dated men when they were in high school, college, or early twenties that fit the "Mr. It." description. These men were tall, athletic, handsome, charismatic, and had promising futures. This dating experience at such a young age set the bar really high for the rest of their lives. And it also created a sense of entitlement and expectation that isn't always realistic. There was an element of innocent nostalgia in their memories, what I call puppy love. Mentally the women made these men into the perfect prototype so new men could never measure up. It is easy to see how men who came along in their adult life were never good enough.

These women clients were accomplished. They were professors, lawyers, and doctors. However, as matching proceeded, the older Mr. It men I interviewed were totally not interested. I couldn't even get them to go on dates. What these women wanted, didn't want them. While professionally and financially successful, these women were not drop-dead gorgeous model types that the Mr. It's wanted. They were just normal, pretty women. These men wanted other options and had different preferences. So these women stay perpetually single because their egos and perceived notions of what they deserve are warped from an early life experience.

Sadly, these expectations cause these women to keep chasing after Mr. It prototype men who don't want them. So they end up being rejected over and over again. They get into situationships with these men, only to be deeply hurt when they realize these men never had long-term intentions for marriage. And often these men will go on to marry someone else causing, even more, pain. As these women age, they start trying to compromise but, by this time, they are insecure and even drive normal good men away.

These women struggle and fluctuate between exaggerated pride and the deep fear they will be single forever. And they treat men accordingly. They tend to treat normal men with a mix of disdain and conceit while trying too hard with the above average men who they are attracted to, eventually pushing them away with obsessive or clingy behavior. So a combined inflated ego and fear keep these women in a vicious single cycle that blocks true love.

Ms. Ego. My next client profile is women who may not have dated the popular guys when they were young. However, they have now obtained a measure of success and feel the pressure to marry a man that matches their status. They want to live up to the expectations of others and greatly care about the perception of others as well. One example is women who try to date and marry men that their parents feel are a great fit. Or they feel competitive with their friends or colleagues and want to impress them. Their choices have nothing to do with love or who is a good match for them and everything to do with trying to please or impress others. Another example is an artistic type who has more of free-flowing spirit and energy, who is not materialistic at all, and who is trying to date and marry a wealthy athlete or businessman. This type of man is typically driven by money and success, not love and causes close to her heart. While she may want to go on missions and serve the community, he is not supportive or interested. They are not a match. Dating with these type of motivations does not attract love.

My type. The next client profile is women who have a very strong "type." What these women have in common is a very clear image of what they believe is a fit for them based on their past experiences. However, this image is not general. Nor is it based on character traits such as integrity, faith, etc. Instead, it is very specific. It typically includes height, income, race, skin complexion, style, profession, and much more. And because this image is so strongly programmed into their psyche it can be very difficult to be open minded to men that don't match the type. Many women create these types based on their fathers or strong male role models. They also tend to have dated or had situationships with at least one or two men that fit this type.

And the fact that they met and interacted with these men is all the proof they need that their "type" exists but they just need to find one that is also loyal and marriage-minded. This goes back to the *Situationship Syndrome* and how we can back ourselves into a very lonely corner when we form these strict requirements around what love should look like. Love is often found with the most unlikely candidates. And remember, the definition of insanity is to keep doing the same thing over and over expecting different results.

The definition of insanity is to keep doing the same thing over and over expecting different results.

The Naysayers. The final group of clients is the Negative Nancy's. They want love desperately yet their thoughts and words sabotage every opportunity for it. They say things like, "There aren't any good men left." And if you think like that then it is your reality. Why date if you believe there aren't any good men left? That means that you are only going to meet bad men because that is all that's available according to your thinking. And because we bring about what we think about that is the exactly what these women receive. When they come to the agency, they have dating horror stories that rival Lifetime movies.

These are my clients that refuse match after match that is presented. They are critical and negative. They find things wrong with every man we recruit, turning down dates, refusing to even meet for coffee or drinks. At the root of the negativity is fear. They have been hurt and are afraid of being hurt more. Their biggest fear is remaining single forever. And this fear translates into becoming pickier and pickier trying to be careful about who they choose in order to not repeat the mistakes of the past. The combined negativity and defensive behavior is not attractive to men and keeps blocking their blessings.

The biggest, overall blessing blocker I see in modern dating, besides ego and fear, is unrealistic expectations when it comes to physical appearance and finances. The average man doesn't come in these perfect packages. In fact, the average man is not super handsome. No matter how much things have changed with traditional gender roles, dating, and marriage, there are some things that haven't changed. God made women be the fairer sex. The average woman is by far prettier than the average man. Research proves this. Below is an excerpt from a study published in 2011 that specifically reported on the percentages of general attractiveness by gender.

> "A majority (56.03%) of the girls are either "attractive" or "very attractive," whereas the comparable figure among boys is much lower (41.75%). In fact, a majority (51.21%) of the boys are "about average." Nearly twice as many girls (19.53%) as boys (10.51%) are "very attractive." It therefore appears that, both in the United Kingdom and the United States, women are indeed more physically attractive on average than men are, at least partly because beautiful parents are, and have been, more likely to have daughters."[15]

The next time you are out and around a lot of people, look around. Make a note of what women look like. And examine the men you see. How many men are over six foot, really handsome, and attractive? And how many beautiful women do you see? If your anecdotal research is anything like mine, it verifies that God has created a system where women are the beautiful creatures. This keeps men chasing us, wanting to marry us, and have babies. It is really that simple. It keeps the species propagating.

And mind you we are just analyzing looks. Take entrepreneurship and education, where women are outdistancing men. We start businesses at twice the rate of men16 and thirty-five percent more women graduate from college than men.[17] Research also shows that women are increasingly less likely to date and marry men with less education than themselves.

The physical preferences many women have, in combination with their other desires like wealth, education, occupation, faith, hobbies or race, literally have them looking for a unicorn. If this is you, a man who fits all your wants and needs is likely either already married, a player, or both. And he is probably so out of your league that, while you are holding out for him, he's dating super models or is so arrogant you wouldn't like him if you did meet him.

There is nothing wrong with preferences, but they don't equal love.

Ladies, I am not trying to discourage you, I am simply giving you the facts to point out how small the pool of men are who will meet all of your requirements. While we women are generally pretty, educated, and starting businesses, the average man is not. Here is a summary of some basics:

- Men over six feet tall in the United States – 14.5%
- Average height of men in the United States – 5'10"
- Men described as "Very Attractive" – 10.51%
- Average income of men over 25 with a High School Degree – $32,307
- Average income of men over 25 with Bachelor's Degree – $62,304
- Men with Bachelor's degrees – 32.3%

As you analyze your own personal desires and requirements in a partner and spouse, consider that many of these desires are not truly necessary. There is nothing wrong with preferences, but they don't equal love.

Most women have not experienced real love. And because we haven't experienced it, we do not have a point of reference. We create all of these requirements because we hope it will equate to love without knowing what real love looks and feels like. When I met my husband, I quickly recognized that the way he loves and cares for me is quite different than any relationship I had previously experienced. He loves me from the crown of my head to the soles of my feet. He is my best friend and has my back through thick and thin.

We create all of these requirements because we hope it will equate to love without knowing what real love looks and feels like.

As I fell in love with him, I realized love trumps any lack of education, income, and physical appearance. This is something I didn't understand when I was single because I had never experienced it. It was only when I dropped my ego and fears, and surrendered to God, that I met the love of my life. I can honestly tell you that, had I met my husband before surrendering to God, I would have rejected him. He was so different from my "requirements" and what I thought I needed and wanted that I wouldn't have even given him a chance.

Here is how my personal blessing blockers would have sabotaged my future happiness. For many years, I avoided and denounced pastors as dating or marriage material. So every time I said, "I will never date a pastor" God was saying ok, you aren't ready for your soulmate. My limited experiences caused me to have limiting thoughts and beliefs that were hindering love. You may say things like, he has to be a least six feet tall, he has to attend church every Sunday, etc. And what you don't realize is that there could be someone perfect for you that is just under six foot tall. Or a man that attends church every other Sunday, but as long as you keep saying these things, you are blocking the arrival of your life partner.

Additionally, my inclination for men making six figures with equal education and business experience would have eliminated my husband. When we met, we had both come through difficult divorces and had struggling businesses. We had the same income, both under six figures. Neither of us had outstanding credit. And we were both about ten pounds overweight. If I hadn't dropped all of my preconceived notions of what Kerry needed to be I would have never met him. Our thoughts and words have that much power over what we receive. I finally got real about who I was, and God blessed me with my perfect match.

He is my mirror image. We both love God. We have the same heart for helping people to heal and prosper. We both love to laugh and have fun. We are quite silly. We are both optimistic, love family, and love to travel. We are attracted to each other and have a chemistry that is through the roof. I have never been more attracted to a man than I am to my husband. And it is not purely physical. It is spiritual and emotional. His love for me and my love for him is a natural aphrodisiac. His kindness, his heart, and his intelligence make him one of the best men I have ever met. And we now make more money and have a better life than we had separately. Together we are better.

When I met him, I knew he was special and different than other men. He was a husband. He was a one-woman man, loyal, and ready to settle down. He hated dating and felt zero need to play the field. All that was missing in his life was the love of a good woman, me! In addition to being successful in many areas, I also recognized his potential to be even greater. I knew he was only scratching the surface of his abilities.

One thing we must understand is that throughout history the majority of men who achieved any level of great success had a love of a woman pushing and propelling him. Being in love with a woman gives men more creativity, focus, and drive. Women are what make average men great. So instead of looking for a perfect man, consider surrendering all of that to God, and opening yourself up to true love where you can grow and excel together.

Here are a few more examples of limiting beliefs that I hear women say quite often that may be blocking love:

- He must be at least six feet tall.
- He must be taller than me.
- He must make more money than me.
- He must be stylish.
- All the good men are married.
- I attract bad men.
- I may stay single forever.

Chapter 7 Reflections:

1. What are some of your Blessing Blockers?
2. How are your thinking and words limiting love?
3. What are you going to do to begin to get out of your own way?
4. How can you begin to get real with yourself and God to live more authentic and genuine?

8

MARRIAGE PREP

Marriage is hard. I know single people tend to romanticize it. Sure, my husband is my soulmate, yet there are moments in our marriage where we have disagreements, we get very frustrated with each other, and it is extremely difficult. We are still two individuals, with expectations, dreams, and feelings that come from different upbringings and experiences. When two people create a merger of their lives it gets messy at times, it is inevitable. And if you aren't in love and best friends it is hard to stick it out.

If you marry for convenience, looks, status, finances, security, or because you got pregnant, you don't love the person, you love the benefits of the person. There is a huge difference. Because if any of those things change, as they often do, you will want out of the marriage. Unfortunately, this is exactly where many people find themselves. They find the most perfect candidate possible who makes them look and feel successful, yet the relationship lacks the legs to survive any storms. Only love can carry you through the struggles of life. You cannot solely rely on your vows or someone's sense of commitment because feelings change with the wind. Only the deepest, truest, no plan B, I can't live-without-you kind of love is going to survive in the 21st Century.

There are too many options, too many reasons to quit, too many easy ways to get a divorce. If you aren't in love, eventually there will be more reasons to leave than there are to stay. Real love is worth the wait, so I encourage you to not settle for less than love because marriage is going to test you. There are so many benefits to love, but it is for mature people. I will write it again; marriage is for mature people. It requires compromise, selflessness, and self-discipline. It requires you to choose your words, choose your battles, and sometimes be quiet when you want to speak. It isn't always going to be your way. Sometimes you must agree to disagree and move forward.

If you aren't in love, eventually there will be more reasons to leave than there are to stay.

- Wife versus Woman -

You cannot control when or how you will meet your future husband. You can't make it happen. You can only prepare and position yourself to be ready to receive him. That's it. That is all you have control over. You are only in control of you. You can't force God's hand by serial dating or not dating at all. You can't fast and pray to make him come faster. It is literally this simple, love comes when you are ready. So the fair question to ask is how do you prepare to be married? The answer is you prepare to be a wife.

A wife is a wife long before she ever gets married.

There are distinct differences between being a woman and being a wife. A wife is a wife long before she ever gets married. So ask yourself, are you a wife? Or are you just a woman? Consider this truth; every woman who is married is not a wife, and every singleton is not just a woman, you simply aren't married yet. Now the strictest definition of a wife is "a married woman: the woman someone is married to."[18] However, I challenge this thinking because we all know there are characteristics of a good wife that are universally beneficial to a man and marriage. So let's examine these characteristics and ask yourself if you currently have them or need to start developing them in preparation for being a wife and having a happy marriage.

We'll start by looking at how scripture describes a wife from Proverbs 18:22, "A good wife is a great blessing to a man, and it is a token of Divine favor."[19] Notice the passage specifies a good wife, not just a woman or any wife, as the blessing. So how do we define her? Below is a list of characteristics that make you an asset to any man. It is about partnership, honor, love, respect, humility, and loyalty. And these same things make a man a great husband. It is reciprocal.

A good wife is a great blessing to a man, and it is a token of Divine favor.

- Be virtuous and dependable.
- Be smart and obtain knowledge.
- Be trustworthy and protect your husband.
- Be faithful and loyal.
- Love your husband and the life you have built together.
- Be an asset, not a liability. Pull your weight and add to the bottom line.

- Work hard and handle your business. Don't be lazy.
- Take care of your family.
- Be kind and giving.
- Make your children respect you.
- Choose your words carefully and use wisdom.

- Husband versus Man -

Just like there are personality traits and characteristics that make a woman ready to be a good wife, there are things that make a man ready to be a good husband. I enlisted the expertise of my pastor husband, who not only gives the male perspective but also gives the perspective of someone who has provided marital counseling to hundreds of couples. His insight into what makes a man ready to take on the responsibility of a wife and/or family, as well as earn the respect of his wife/family for being a good man is as follows:

> *He is emotionally and spiritually mature.*

1. He is emotionally and spiritually mature.
2. He is a good communicator.
3. He is responsible.
4. He is experienced.
5. He is in love.
6. He is hard working.
7. He is done playing.

In addition to these characteristics, I have observed that men who commit and fall in love have some other things in common. He feels the woman loves him for who he is and not for what he owns.

He feels she is the best woman he will ever have and is afraid of losing her. He feels accepted because he can be himself and share his deepest thoughts and feelings. He feels secure to give her his heart, and she will not hurt him. He feels she brings out the best in him and adds value. He feels she completes him and complements him in a way that makes for a great partnership.

> *He feels she brings out the best in him and adds value.*

Chapter 8 Reflections:

1. Are you a wife or a woman?
2. What areas do you need to work on to become ready for marriage?
3. When you analyze what makes a man ready and a good husband, how will this affect your dating choices?

9

DATING AND WAITING

While most women want to be married, they are not actively dating. They may have the occasional date, but they are not positioning themselves to meet men consistently. Yes, even after you've done the work of healing, accepting your blessings, and becoming marriage-minded wife material, there is more to do to actually meet these men once you're ready. Therefore, it's vital you begin adapting to modern dating. I call this Dating and Waiting because as you begin to date, you must still be patient while waiting to meet that special man.

Many women don't like that they have to get proactive about this process. Many are lazy when it comes to dating because, historically, we are used to men doing everything – initiating, pursuing, planning, following-up, courting, and proposing. We hate being on dating sites, we hate having to position ourselves, we hate that men don't approach as much, we hate having to work at it at all, which is why so many women remain single. The women I know that are meeting and dating great men have embraced the new ways of meeting men.

You must be willing to meet men halfway. Position yourself to meet men and reciprocate interest and intent. This *requires* you being open to virtual introductions. Recall my estimate that seven out of ten connections for long-term relationships are happening virtually. You cannot afford to narrow your options to the occasional random man you meet when out or the occasional referral from a friend. Both men and your friends are too consumed with their own busy lives to be worrying about approaching you or your love life. This means you are responsible for positioning yourself for love.

> *Position yourself to meet men and reciprocate interest and intent.*

- Online Dating Prep -

So welcome to dating in the 21st Century. There are all different types of people online, but online dating is a process. It requires patience, diligence, and a strategy. Here is a short version of my very best online dating advice for you:

1. If you do not have professional pictures – and I don't mean a corporate headshot or church directory photo – get some. Your pictures are EVERYTHING.
2. Get two looks in your pictures, a "Dressy Date Night" look in a dress and heels, and a "Casual Date" look with jeans and a tee or jacket. Always in high heels. The goal is sophisticated, sexy, and fun. Show your personality in your photos. Smile. And make sure your outfits accentuate your body type and assets. These two looks are a preview of what you look like on a date and men are very visual. You need a close up of your face and one picture that shows your body. Again, these are not your work or church

clothes. You need dating clothes.

3. Choose the largest dating site whether free or paid. You want to be fishing in the largest pond possible.
4. Upload your two best pictures from your shoot. One of your dressy look and one of your casual look. Two to three pictures max! More is not better.
5. When you write your profile keep it short and sweet. Write it to attract your male best friend. Be honest but make sure it is fun, upbeat, and positive. People date for fun and to enjoy themselves. DO NOT write about what you don't want, about bad dating experiences, or anything negative. That is not FUN. Write about your hobbies, what makes you happy, and what you enjoy.
6. When you start receiving messages, understand that ninety percent of them will be from men you are not even halfway interested in. Delete those messages.
7. Only respond to messages from men who meet some very basic compatibility points.
8. Discover more in phone conversations and dates.
9. First dates are simply an interview for a second date. A second date is an interview for a third, etc.
10. Have fun!

- First Date Protocol -

Let's dig deeper on first date best practices, so you're making the most of your efforts and time.

1. Dating attire should always put your best foot forward. Whether dressy or casual, wear clothes that are comfortable yet flattering. Research shows we make up our minds about people within four seconds of seeing them. That is how important first impressions are in dating. Put effort into your appearance because you want the same from your date. If you need help, hire a style consultant to create a new look. Invest in a makeover if necessary. Invest in yourself to be first date ready.

2. Dress for your body type. Accentuate your assets. If you have great legs, show them. Don't wear a dress down to your ankles. If you have a great waist, accentuate it with a belt. This is all about showing off what you have! Mutual attraction is imperative. It can be the hardest part of connecting with people, so looking good is not an option. Sweats and ponytails will come later.

3. Be confident, it is so sexy. This is one of the reasons we encourage you to dress great for dates. If you love how you look, it creates more confidence. Never wear clothes that make you feel self-conscious or uncomfortable, it will distract you throughout the date. You won't be able to relax or be yourself.

> *Be confident, it is so sexy.*

4. Self-Love in dating. The best way to practice self-love while dating is boundaries and speaking your truth. Learning to express your likes and dislikes emphasizes that your voice and feelings matter. Examples of this are letting a man know when he isn't pleasing you or has done something that you don't like. "You teach people how to treat you by what you allow, what you stop, and what you reinforce."[20]

> *You teach people how to treat you by what you allow, what you stop, and what you reinforce.*

5. ***First dates are always in a public place.*** Not someone's home or a friend's house. You are meeting a stranger. You don't know this person yet. Take your time.
6. ***Make first dates as casual as possible, such as coffee, ice cream, dessert, a walk in the park, or roller skating.*** Anything that allows for a casual meet-up without locking you into spending hours with someone you may or may not like once you spend time with them.
7. ***Always meet them there and drive your own car.*** This is in case the date doesn't go well, and you want to leave. Or if someone is rude.
8. ***Discussing exes is off limits on a first date.*** These dates should be fun and intriguing, they are not therapy sessions. Hopefully, you already dropped all your baggage but, if your date starts going down that path, politely change the subject.
9. ***Ask important questions to get to know people***. Questions like are they happy and what are their goals, purpose, and passions? These all help you better evaluate if you two are going in the same direction.
10. ***Do a chemistry test.*** Is he kissable? On a first date, this is the *only* question you should ask yourself as it pertains to physical attraction. When you look at them, are you attracted enough to their energy and spirit to see yourself kissing them eventually? If they pass this test and you like everything else about them, you should go on a second date. If not, you shouldn't waste your time.

- Best Dating Practices -

Use these best practices and boundaries to help you remain focused and balanced during the dating phase. Over the years of matching and coaching, these guidelines have been very helpful in steering clients who date for the purpose of marriage.

1. ***Develop a dating strategy to meet people.*** Make yourself available. This should be a combination of online dating, networking events, and social groups. I recommend all of them, not just one, to have a well-rounded strategy.
2. ***Be aware and in the moment.*** At the grocery store, doctor's office, gym, mall, and gas station. Instead of being on your phone with your head down, look up. Make eye contact. Be aware of your surroundings. Men are everywhere, and you never know how you are going to meet your husband and soulmate.
3. ***You should date more than one person at a time.*** These are essentially friends you are getting to know. The majority of men you meet are dating other women simultaneously. You should too. This keeps you balanced and less emotional until a man steps up to take you off the market.
4. ***Dating more than one person does not make you promiscuous.*** You need to be vetting and qualifying multiple men without having sex. Until a man makes it clear that he wants to be in a committed relationship with you, never stop dating others.
5. ***Some people aren't photogenic and don't have great pictures.*** So if you are meeting through a dating site or matchmaker, don't write someone off because their pictures are just okay. They may knock your socks off in person.
6. ***Talk on the phone a few times before agreeing to a date.*** If

there isn't any chemistry on the phone, don't waste your time meeting in person. Talking and communicating is the basic building block of a relationship. If it doesn't flow on the phone, it isn't going anywhere. Talking and communicating is not rocket science when it comes to soulmates. It is like breathing, so make sure you don't try to force this because it should just happen naturally.

7. ***Don't chase people.*** If you are doing all the initiating, then the other person isn't really interested. It has to be mutual. Calling and texting are easy when you like someone. A great way to think about it is we all have the same twenty-four hours in a day. If someone doesn't choose to text or call you sometime during those twenty-four hours, they likely aren't thinking about you, and you aren't a priority.

8. Focus on the health of relationships. We often ask clients about the overall health of all their relationships, not just romantic ones. The quality of a person's relationships is a great indicator of their personal emotional health. If someone struggles to have healthy relationships with friends and family, they are likely the contributing factor. Beware of people who have not worked on their own issues and show an unwillingness to do so.

9. Ask questions and be a great listener. I find most people, especially women, don't ask enough questions while dating. Ask questions, many of them, and listen to what men say and also what they don't say. This is the vetting process. If you have been dating for a while and they never talk about your future together, it is likely they aren't thinking about a future with you. People talk about what they are thinking.

10. Men who date with the purpose of finding a wife have a lot of questions. He is vetting you too. Men who don't ask a lot of questions are not trying to get to know you. This is a simple sign of someone's basic intentions and whether they are interested in a long-term relationship. If they initially ask questions and then stop, they have lost interest and are no longer vetting you.

Men who date with the purpose of finding a wife have a lot of questions.

11. Be intentional. Let potential daters know very early you are dating with purpose, you have enough friends, and you are seeking your soulmate. Be clear that you have worked hard to be truly ready for love and commitment. It's not saying they are The One. However, it will make it clear you are not looking for casual dating and flings. For the man who wants the same, this will help them know where you stand and they will typically communicate if they are at the same stage in life. For the players, it will likely scare them off which is good.

12. Verify their life stage. If you want marriage and children, don't date someone who emphatically doesn't want kids. This is non-negotiable if you really want a family. If someone is still hanging out in clubs every weekend, they likely still love single life. If they are inconsistent with communication or availability, they aren't making getting to know you a priority. These are all signs they aren't looking to settle down or are simply not interested in you. Either way, keep it moving.

If they are inconsistent with communication or availability, they aren't making getting to know you a priority.

13. Dating long distance can be dangerous. You have to be careful when dating long distance to not move too fast. You still need to vet him. You still need to date and have experiences to get to know him. Phone conversations do not equate to time spent.

14. Confirm a common faith. It is very important you have a shared faith system and values. This forms the foundation of your relationship.

15. Pray about each person you meet. Ask for insight and for God to reveal who they really are. After you ask, pay attention to the details.

16. Watch your body language. It is important to open your spirit to love and allow this energy to shine through in your body language. On dates and out in public, make eye contact. Smile. Give compliments. Initiate conversations. Saying hello to someone is a great place to start.

17. Most dating experiences will be with strangers who you've just met. It is imperative you get to know this person. Conversation and activities are a must. If a person is not interested in talking and going out with you then, no matter what they say, they are not seriously interested in you. ***Nobody is perfect.*** When listening to where someone is at in life look at the big picture. Evaluate the whole person. Take into account their values, heart, integrity, work ethic, and other positive characteristics.

18. No more dating purely on potential. We are not in high school or college anymore. You are dating a real person, not an ideal or fairy tale. If you can't love someone for where they are at or who they are, leave them alone. True love isn't based on what someone might become or might do.

19. Be very slow to go over to their house or invite them to yours. This is one of the fastest ways to move into the forbidden gray area that can lead to sex or a situationship. It is also one of the reasons there isn't more dating and courting versus "hanging out." Maintain boundaries around your personal space until you are in a commitment.

20. No meeting your kids until you are in a committed relationship. It is an honor only suited for men you are going to the next level with in life. It's entirely plausible to date someone for two weeks, discover a complete deal-breaker, and never speak to them again. You don't want to drag your kids into this process. Only the deserving get the honor of meeting your family.

21. Sex is absolutely not an option before commitment. Wives do not have sex with random men. If you want to be a wife, it is time to start acting like it no matter what you have practiced previously. Date with the purpose of marriage.

22. People you date are not your boyfriend or partner. They are strangers who you are getting to know to see if they have potential to become a best friend, partner, and husband.

People you date are not your boyfriend or partner.

23. Having the commitment conversation. If you are interested in exclusively dating someone and he hasn't initiated the conversation, ask him about his feelings and intention. Only do this in person and pay attention to his body language. If he gets really uncomfortable, gets fidgety, and won't give you a clear answer then he doesn't feel the same. Do not date someone indefinitely without discovering if it is mutual.

24. Boundaries for sex later in the relationship. If you are not steadfast in waiting until marriage for sex, you must at least wait until there is a committed relationship. We emphasize this over and over again with clients. While we believe God's way of waiting for marriage is healthiest, being monogamous and exclusive first will save you a lot of emotional turmoil and false intimacy with people you barely know or people who aren't looking for true love. Letting someone know you don't have sex without commitment sends a clear message. However, once you say it, you must stick to it.

25. Sex is not a topic for casual dating. If you are celibate, do not talk about this on the first few dates. These are strangers. You don't talk about your sex life with strangers. That is a topic reserved for men you are more deeply interested in, and it is mutual.

26. A committed relationship is when both parties mutually and verbally agree to only see each other. This technically begins the courting phase as long as you both want marriage and a long-term relationship.

> *A committed relationship is when both parties mutually and verbally agree to only see each other.*

Chapter 9 Reflections:

1. How do you need to adjust your dating strategy?
2. What are your first steps?
3. What bad habits do you need to overcome?
4. What new boundaries do you need to establish?

10

MARRY
ING
YOUR
SOULMATE

So you've put the work in on yourself, your dating strategy, your relationship, and you're with someone special. How do you determine if he is your soulmate? How do you know when you're ready for marriage? And how do you establish a happy union once you are married? Getting you to and through these milestones is my ultimate goal for you and your journey, so let's walk through them.

- Identifying Your Soulmate -

For some, recognizing a soulmate is easy, like breathing or lightening striking. For others, a slower recognition process occurs, which does not mean the soulmate is any less of a soulmate. Sometimes a little help or prodding is needed in this identification process, so let's now examine some common traits of a soulmate relationship.

1. **You may or may not feel an immediate strong physical attraction for your soulmate however you will feel a strong pull or connection.** He is still kissable, just don't expect there to be off-the-charts chemistry. Sometimes this is more of a slow simmer, but you will feel a connection that keeps you wanting to see him.

2. Communication will flow effortlessly. You will be able to talk and talk and talk. In person, on the phone, text, all of the above. It is like meeting your best friend.

3. Unconditional love. When you are around him, you will feel safe and accepted very early on. You will feel a deep sense of peace.

4. Flaws and all. There will be a feeling he understands you and just "gets you." You will feel completely comfortable just being yourself. Your soulmate accepts all of you, flaws included.

5. Your soulmate will stretch you and motivate you to be the truest and most authentic version of yourself. The relationship will encourage you to accomplish and pursue your purpose and passion in a new way.

You may or may not feel an immediate strong physical attraction for your soulmate however you will feel a strong pull or connection.

6. Ride or die. You will have the feeling that it is "us against the world." That you are partners in life.

7. He will enhance your life. He will make life better in many ways. He will bring more joy, peace, laughter, and fun to your life.

8. Never loved liked this. When you fall for your soulmate, it will make you feel like you have never been in love before. It is deeper and more connected than anything you have experienced previously. Cheating and divorce will be foreign concepts.

9. Supernatural love. There is a feeling that it is not just natural but supernatural. Together you will have more power, more problem-solving abilities, and more success reaching goals.

10. Strong chemistry. Chemistry will become very intense as the relationship develops. Soulmate relationships are passionate. This doesn't mean it will always be smooth. The passionate nature of the relationship can often cause intense disagreements, however leaving and/or divorce isn't an option.

11. Fulfilled. There is a deep sense of fulfillment.

- Your Marriage Prep Checklist -

Identifying whether you are personally ready to get married often happens in conjunction with other phases during a committed relationship. Therefore don't think of this checklist as something to be used only *after* you identify your soulmate, it should be used *during* a committed relationship, including the soulmate identification phase.

So the big question. Are *you* ready to get married? Using this checklist tool will help you evaluate yourself before marriage. It also serves as a guide for working on areas that need improvement:

1. Are you a good communicator? Do you express your feelings and thoughts in a logical way? Or do you internalize and then explode in moments of anger? Do you expect your significant other to be a mind reader? Do you give people the silent treatment instead of communicating your needs and desires? Learning good communication skills is necessary for a healthy marriage.

2. Are you willing to compromise? Does everything have to be your way all the time? Do you pout, mope, or give the silent treatment when things don't go your way? Marriage is for grown-ups. It requires maturity to commit your life to another human being. And you must be willing to compromise and sometimes even agree to disagree.

3. Are you done playing around? Have you enjoyed your single life? Have you dated, had fun, and explored people, places, and things? Curiosity is often a dangerous element that can sabotage great relationships. If you know there is nothing and no one else who compares to your spouse and the life you've built, you are less likely to be tempted to cheat, leave, or feel like you are missing out on anything.

4. Are you healthy and ready for a life-long commitment? Have you dealt with your issues or are you ignoring the self-work that needs to be done? You cannot afford to ignore your issues. Your issues will only get amplified in a relationship. And you don't want to be the unhealthy half of a relationship. It is your job to get healthy and healed. Your spouse is only there to support you. Happiness is an inside job that is between you and God.

5. Do you know who you are? Have you taken the time to get to know yourself? Your needs, wants, and direction in life? What are your greatest desires? This is a crucial question because, if you are unsure, then your desires could change. Choosing a spouse who fits you before you know the answers to these questions can have you connecting with someone who is all wrong for you. While you are single, take the time to focus on yourself. Get deeply honest and explore your "Why." Get in touch with the deeper meaning of your life, and this will facilitate meeting a spouse who is aligned with you on a much deeper level.

6. Are you crazy in love? I mean truly in love. Marriage is going to test you. If you aren't in love, don't even think about it. We no longer live in the era of people marrying for land, inheritance, and titles. Nor do we live in a time where you marry for survival. In the 21st Century, there are too many options, too many distractions. You are going to need more than wedding vows and commitment to hold a marriage together. You need love. So if you are contemplating marriage right now because the person is a really good person, but you aren't crazy in love, think again. You should not have a Plan B when you are getting married.

7. Do you really know the person…under many different circumstances? Before you consider marrying someone, you need to know what and who you are committing. Have you seen them angry, disappointed, or sad? Have you seen them experience losing? Everyone is great when they are winning but how someone handles defeat will tell you a lot. Who you marry is one of the most important decisions you will ever make in your life. Take your time. Get to know the person. You wouldn't go into business with just anyone so you shouldn't enter into marriage lightly. This is your life. It is a crucial decision. Research shows your choice in a spouse is one of the biggest factors for success. You are literally making a choice that can make or break you.

8. Do you have common goals and vision? Are you going in the same direction in life? Marriage is a partnership and, just like any business partnership, there has to be common vision and goals for it to succeed. Partners can't be going in different directions. And if you do find you have two different visions, there has to be synergy and compatibility between these visions. You have to be able to support each other's goals without jeopardizing your own dreams and the relationship.

9. Do you have doubts or unanswered questions? You need to be sure. And you can't afford to ignore any doubts or red flags. Make sure you talk to your future spouse with honesty. He needs to be your best friend and soulmate. Ask questions and pay attention to the answers.

10. Are you at peace? Cultivate your personal peace. This will help you go slow in dating and be sensitive to the nudges and guidance from God in committing to the right man. It will also help you in your relationship and marriage.

- Establishing a Happy Marriage -

After confirming you and your partner are soulmates, and you both have the characteristics that make you marriage-ready, how do you ensure it's a happy marriage? I'll share my own list that aided me as a newlywed, and continues to do so, in building a godly partnership.

Things I DON'T expect from my husband:

- To solve all my problems, he's not God.
- To make me happy, that's my responsibility.
- To heal all my broken places, once again, he's not God.
- To pay for everything. Why would I need him to do that when I make money too? And if he pays for everything, there's a bunch of stuff he's going to want me to do that I don't want to HAVE TO DO (i.e., cook and clean ever day!) I only want to cook twice a week, eat out, and get a cleaning person.

Things I DO expect from my husband:

- To be my best friend.
- To be faithful and loyal.
- To help me solve problems.
- To add to my happiness.
- To support and love me when I'm hurting.
- To pray for me and believe in me.
- To hold me when I need to cry.
- To share the work in our home.

- To add to and not subtract from the great life we've worked so hard to create.
- Fun and companionship.
- To never leave and always have my back, even when life throws throws us some tough times.
- To bring me coffee in bed every morning. Kidding…not really.

This list is a good start to what a happy marriage in the 21st Century can look like when both people work together. Healthy expectations and an equal division of labor, love, and companionship create a partnership. Don't forget the coffee!

Chapter 10 Reflections:

1. Review the ways to identify your soulmate. Keep them in mind when dating. It will help to simplify the dating process.
2. Review the Marriage Prep Checklist for the areas you need improvement.
3. Make a plan to take action for improvement.

CONCLUSION:
GOD HAS A LOVE STORY FOR YOU

Every love story is unique and different. Love has more to do with timing, readiness, and positioning than anything else. I believe every person has an appointment with love. Just like how I met Kerry through a picture on Facebook, I believe you have an appointed time to meet your soulmate. Just like my clients and my own journey, it is *your* responsibility to be ready and intentional about love. God will lead you to the right opportunities and the right people however you must seize them and not allow fear to hold you back. It is going to require you to step out of your comfort zone.

When I look back at the timing of meeting Kerry, I can honestly say that God began turning up the heat on me, so I was ready to meet him. I had procrastinated and dragged my feet long enough. Once I started pursuing my purpose and positioned myself to give and receive love, I invited it and Kerry into my life.

And I know that God has the same for you. I am not special. I am just a woman who surrendered to God. Throughout my entire time being single, there is one scripture I always read, and it gave me courage that my soulmate, my promise, was real and was waiting for me. As you begin dating and putting into practice what

I have shared in this book, I pray this scripture helps you hold on too. Be patient. God is with you, and He is using every lesson and situation for your good. He loves you, and I love you too.

> ***"For I know the plans I have for you," says the Lord. "They are plans for good and not for disaster, to give you a future and a hope."***
> Jeremiah 29:11 NLT

EPILOGUE

MY 21ST CENTURY LOVE STORY

I met my husband, Kerry through Facebook. About three months prior I was introduced to a woman through a mutual associate about possibly doing a reality show on women who are in ministry and business. We didn't do the show, but she and I took a liking to each other and would occasionally meet. We went to lunch and shopping one day, and she said the infamous words, "let's take a selfie!" She took the picture, tagged me, and posted it on Facebook. A few days later, she popped into my Facebook Messenger inbox to tell me that her friend "liked me." My first thought was "Who is this friend?" She had never mentioned him before, and she knew I was single, so I was a little skeptical. I asked her about him, and she told me he was a pastor. I didn't run for the hills like I would have a year or two before (reference the Blessing Blockers chapter). I was open to *at least* seeing a picture. She sent his picture via Messenger, and he was really handsome! *Sidebar: Friends tend to introduce you to the men in their circles that are the leftovers and those they haven't dated or slept with. Not always reliable referrals. This was more organic and random since he had done the initiating.*

I gave her permission to give him my number, and he called

me within an hour. During that very first conversation, I told him very sweetly I was dating with the purpose of marriage, and I had enough friends so if he wasn't at the same place, I didn't want to waste our time. He said he was never much of a dater and he was a one woman man. *Sidebar: I had learned to get very straightforward with men because men who are serious and like you will appreciate your candor and men who just want to play will go away.* So we were in agreement that we were on the same page. That was a Tuesday. We talked several times that day and every day after. We then decided to meet that Friday.

Friday comes, and I am excited to meet this man. Our conversations revealed a humble man with family values and integrity. I arrive at Atlantic Station in downtown Atlanta, Georgia and park. We agreed to meet at a trendy restaurant that has an outdoor patio I love. I arrive, I see across the street a tall, handsome man standing in the restaurant's front door with the biggest smile. I walk to meet him, and his smile is contagious. By the time I'm at the door, we're both starting to laugh because we are smiling so much. I ask him why he is standing outside and he said "waiting on you."

It may seem like a small thing, but no man had ever done that. To me, it seemed he was so excited to meet me that he couldn't wait even a few more minutes inside the restaurant. I loved it! I loved his honesty and transparency, he wasn't trying to play it cool. He wasn't trying to hide his excitement. He opened the door for me as we entered (this would be the first of many doors, Kerry is a southern gentleman who opens all the doors, including putting me in and out of the car every time we go somewhere). The hostess seats us on the patio. Kerry and I sit next to each other at the table instead of across from each other. You would have never known this was our first date and first time meeting each other. It felt like we had known each other our whole lives. He honestly felt like family. At a certain point, while talking, I touched his leg, and we were both very aware of that touch. Our chemistry was undeniable and off the charts! We ordered our food and talked, talked, talked. And our hands had a way of continuing to make contact with each other in small touches and gestures. He had been through a really hard divorce, and I could feel the residual pain. I am very intuitive and empathetic, so I feel things very strongly about people. Kerry was no exception. As we finished eating, a storm began rolling in, so we decided to move inside to wait it out. We both knew we weren't ready for the date to end.

We sat at the bar and talked more while the storm raged – thunder, lightning, and crazy wind. (See first date picture) When I look back, I say that the storm was nature reacting to Kerry and me meeting each other for the first time. As we sat there for hours, the feeling of knowing each other for a long time became stronger, and we still weren't ready to leave each other. It was a magnetism that was is hard to describe. I knew it was different and special. I really liked him.

When it was time to leave, he walked me to my car. He reached for a hug. After the hug, as we were pulling back, we were still holding each other, and I kissed him! You read that right, I KISSED HIM! Right on the mouth. Just a peck but still a kiss. His eyes got so big, and we started laughing. He couldn't believe I had kissed him on the first date. I don't think the pastor had ever had anyone kiss him on the first date and it definitely wasn't my habit. However, I know a lot of people nowadays sleep together the first time they meet someone. I had never done that or understood how people get intimate so fast, but my first date with Kerry helped me to understand how it can happen because our chemistry was that strong. And do not look at me sideways girls, I know exactly what's going on out here in the streets. People are sleeping together so fast which is why it is so expected and accepted as the norm. I do not endorse it, but it's real.

After that first date, I knew I wasn't letting Kerry go. He didn't know it yet, but I knew. He was worth taking the time to get to know! He was a catch! Kerry is a very humble man. He didn't live in the city so was never corrupted by dating lots of people. He was different. He had never done online dating. He wasn't into social media. He didn't realize his own worth or how rare he is, but I did. He is smart, handsome, talented, spiritually grounded, with a huge heart for helping people. I had finally met my twin, my soulmate and I knew it WAY BEFORE HE DID. He was a little slower girls.

Kerry courted me. He was never much of a dater and had zero pretenses or game. We spent long hours on the phone talking. He made time to see me A LOT. I had been talking to a couple of men when I met Kerry, but as he preoccupied more and more of my mind and time, the other men ceased to exist to me. We lived about an hour away from each other, and I told him when we met that I am not big on driving. He would drive an hour each way to take me out. *Sidebar: Over the years of dating, I learned to ask for what I want and let my preferences be known. Men that really like you will do it and men that don't, won't.* Our dates consisted of brunch, picnics, ice cream, movies, and bowling. We had fun doing simple things. We had only been dating for a couple weeks when I began picking up on a lot more residual pain from his divorce than I had originally detected. I began feeling like he wasn't completely healed, so I talked to him about it.

Our discussion revealed a lot of pain in his past. The pressures of being a pastor had taken its toll on his life. The expectations

of people for him to be a great man of God had never allowed him to just be Kerry. So I suggested that he take my "Healed to Love Course," after all, this is what I do as a coach and matchmaker. I help people recover and heal for the purpose of love. I said if we wanted any chance of our relationship working, we both had to be as healed and healthy as possible. And that I thought we should focus more on our friendship because as a friend I could see he was hurting and I didn't want to ignore that. He agreed, so we put our dating on hold while he completed the course. He took it very seriously too. He was on time for his appointments, did his homework, and sat on my couch and talked to me just like a client.

Kerry's willingness to do this really impressed me because it showed his willingness to work on himself and openness to improvement. He didn't allow pride to keep him from getting the help he needed. Before you run out and start dating for potential, Kerry's pros outweighed his cons. His life was very settled with minimal drama. Although not rich he was financially secure and great with money. He was pastoring his own church for over twelve years with thirty years of experience in ministry. His car was paid for, and he had minimal debt. He is the leader of his family. He cares for his mother and siblings. He is a great father. He is wise, patient, and a gentleman. In other words, besides hurting from ministry and his divorce he is a great guy! No one is perfect, so you have to make sure that someone's flaws are manageable and compatible with you.

Kerry's imperfections were perfectly matched to me. I could help him to be better by just being my natural self. Healthy relationships complement each other in this way. That is the kind of person you can work with and grow together. It also proved how much I already loved Kerry because I never thought I would coach my potential husband. In my ideal scenario, any man I would date would be emotionally healthy already. So my patience and willingness to help him revealed the depth of my love for him. And it still does to this day. I have never been as patient with someone as I am with Kerry. This is what love does.

Kerry helped me too. About a year before meeting Kerry, my mother died from cancer. She fought for ten years. I had not really grieved my mother. As many of you can probably relate, I tend to just keep working and focusing on everyone else and not my own feelings, and in this case my own grief. There were moments when Kerry would hug me and not let go as I cried and cried. He just knew that was what I needed and I was safe with him to do it. Kerry is naturally caring and compassionate so comforting me and helping me grieve came naturally to him. Kerry became my rock, my best friend, my safe place. With him, I could just be Rebecca. Not Rebecca the coach, the leader, the healer, the matchmaker... just me. I could be vulnerable and just have my moment. I could also be silly and fun. We were like two peas in a pod, and we became inseparable.

We met each other's families, and we all got along great. We dated for about twelve months when we began to talk about marriage. I was enjoying the courting so much and getting to know him that time just flew by. We wanted to elope, but our family and friends begged us to have a small ceremony. So after sixteen, right before Christmas, we were married in his small church with an intimate group of family and friends in attendance. It was a beautiful, simple ceremony. We went home afterward, ate our wedding cake, and prepared for Christmas with our children. This is my 21st Century love story.

NOTES

1. Fairy tale definition (n.d.). Retrieved from https://en.oxforddictionaries.com/definition/fairy_tale

2. Coontz, S. (2006). Marriage, a history: How love conquered marriage. New York, New York: Penguin Books

3. Coontz, S. (2006). Marriage, a history: How love conquered marriage. New York, New York: Penguin Books

4. Coontz, S. (2006). Marriage, a history: How love conquered marriage. New York, New York: Penguin Books

5. Women's History in America (n.d.). Retrieved from http://www.wic.org/misc/history.htm

6. Women's History in America (n.d.). Retrieved from http://www.wic.org/misc/history.htm

7. Marcus, B. (2015). True Feminism is About Equality for Both Genders. Retrieved from http://www.forbes.com/sites/bonniemarcus/2015/03/31/true-feminism-is-about-equality-for-both-genders

8. Chang, L. (2015). Americans Spend an Alarming Amount of Time Checking Social Media on Their Phones. Retrieved from http://www.digitaltrends.com/mobile/informate-report-social-media-smartphone-use

9. Online Dating Statistics (2016). Retrieved from http://www.statisticbrain.com/online-dating-statistics/

10. Online Dating Statistics (2016). Retrieved from http://www.statisticbrain.com/online-dating-statistics/

11. Kurtz, A. (2013). Why 26% of U.S. Women Still Choose to

Not Work. Retrieved from http://money.cnn.com/2013/08/13/news/economy/women-work-force/

12. Neal, A. (2014). 9 Signs You Are in a Situationship. Retrieved from http://aidanneal.com/2014/08/06/9-signs-youre-situationship/

13. Khoshaba, D. (2012). A Seven Step Prescription for Self-Love. Retrieved from https://www.psychologytoday.com/blog/get-hardy/201203/seven-step-prescription-self-love

14. Barry, M. (2011). The forgiveness project: The startling discovery of how to overcome cancer, find health, and achieve peace. Grand Rapids, MI: Kregel Publications.

15. Kanazawa, S. (2011). Women Are More Beautiful Than Men: Natural selection has its own logic. Retrieved from https://www.psychologytoday.com/blog/the-scientific-fundamentalist/201101/women-are-more-beautiful-men

16. Oppenheimer Funds (2016). Women Start Up New Businesses at Twice the Rate of Men. Retrieved from https://www.oppenheimerfunds.com/investors/article/women-start-up-new-businesses-at-twice-the-rate-of-men

17. Birger, J. (2015). Date-onomics: How Dating Became a Lopsided Numbers Game. New York: Workman Publishing.

18. Wife definition (1828). Retrieved from https://www.merriam-webster.com/dictionary/wife

19. Proverbs 18:22, Matthew Henry Commentary

20. Gaskins, T. (2013, January 16). You teach people how to treat you by what you allow, what you stop, and what you reinforce. Know that! [Tweet]. Retrieved from https://twitter.com/tonygaskins/status/291748201919295488?lang=en

ACKNOWLEDGEMENTS

God, I thank you. I am grateful for my journey and your never-ending love towards me.

There are so many people that have been a part of not just this project but my life.

Kerry A. Pope, for his patience and love through my daily ups and downs. Your love anchors me and give me the strength and courage to keep going.

Charles and Linda Crockrell, my parents. Your unconditional love and support has helped me become the woman I am today. Mom, every day you told me that I could accomplish anything I put my mind to in life. That singular truth has given me the courage to never quit and believe in myself.

And for my boys, Vashaun, Savion, and Jeven. Thank you for being my why and that push for greatness. Thank you for always believing in your mom.

Simone Darlington, you are my best friend, girl soulmate, and book designer. You have been a rock and constant support. You challenge me and set me straight at times. You are more than my friend, you are my sister. Thank you for believing in me through some of the hardest times of my life. And thank you for capturing exactly what I wanted for the book cover and interior design.

Rachel Fikes, my childhood friend and editor, you are a God-send. Thank you for your sacrifice and diligence to help perfect this book.

Georgia Steele, thank you for all your help with reading and feedback.

Kya Muhammad, thank you for your unwavering support and love.

Vangi Caver, thank you for you inspiration for the color scheme of the book.

Halliday Donaldson, thank you for your PR services and promotions.

Cheryl Allen Clark, for your personal dedication to Godly Girls and myself. Thank you.

To all of my clients, the Godly Girls, the Divine Dreamers Circle, friends and family around the world, thank you for your part in my journey. And for all of your love and support.

ABOUT THE AUTHOR

Rebecca Lynn is a certified spiritual, life, and relationship coach, as well as a matchmaker. Her passion is helping people to heal in order to receive God's best in every area of life. She is the founder of the Godly Girls Club, an organization for with thousands of members around the world. Godly Girls are women of faith with the mission of Power, Love, and Purpose. Additionally, she is the founder of the Divine Dreamers Circle where she works personally with women to manifest abundant life.

Rebecca Lynn is married to her soulmate and best friend, Kerry A. Pope. And has three very big sons that she adores. She is the President of The Pope Agency, a faith-based coaching & counseling firm in Atlanta, GA that she founded with her husband. Together they coach and counsel women and couples both nationally and internationally.

Combining her love of coaching and teaching, Rebecca Lynn loves helping people on their journey to abundant life and love. She is also the author of Dare to Dream: A Manifesting Manual that she offers as a free download at www.godlygirlsclub.com

You can follow Rebecca Lynn Pope on social media at the following:
IG: @rebeccalynnpope
FB: @matchmakeruncut
TW: @rebeccalynnpope

Made in the USA
Middletown, DE
06 November 2020

23434200R00097